# Repentance—Good News!

*Repentance—Good News!* is translated from the French published by Éditions Olivétan as *La repentance, une bonne nouvelle*.

In the same collection of translations:

*The Silence of God during the Passion*
*Praying the Psalms*
*Spiritual Maladies*
*The Tenderness of God*
*Becoming a Disciple*
*From Darkness to Light*

# Repentance—Good News!

Daniel Bourguet

Foreword by Bob Ekblad

Translated from the French

CASCADE *Books* · Eugene, Oregon

REPENTANCE—GOOD NEWS!

Cascade Books
An Imprint of Wipf and Stock Publishers
199 W. 8th Ave., Suite 3
Eugene, OR 97401

www.wipfandstock.com

PAPERBACK ISBN: 978-1-4982-8170-6
HARDCOVER ISBN: 978-1-4982-8172-0
EBOOK ISBN: 978-1-4982-8171-3

*Cataloguing-in-Publication data:*

Names: Bourguet, Daniel.

Title: Repentance—Good News! / Daniel Bourguet.

Description: Eugene, OR: Cascade Books, 2016 | Includes bibliographical references.

Identifiers: ISBN 978-1-4982-8170-6 (paperback) | ISBN 978-1-4982-8172-0 (hardcover) | ISBN 978-1-4982-8171-3 (ebook)

Subjects: LSCH: Repentance — Christianity | Repentance — biblical teaching | Old Testament — influence |

*Classification: BS680.R45 B65 2016 (print) | BS680.R45 (ebook)*

Manufactured in the USA.                                      10/04/16

# Contents

# Translator's Note

IN SOME INSTANCES THERE are idioms in French that are difficult to translate, but that has not generally been the case with this book. The author's original notes and references are all to French works or translations, and it has not always been possible to provide equivalent references in English. Further to the author's original notes some translator's notes have been added as footnotes, generally as glosses of the French, sometimes of a more explanatory nature; in every instance these notes have been checked with the author. Biblical passages are mostly the translator's version of the French since at times the point would be lost if this were not so; the author chooses freely among French translations.

# Foreword

THE PUBLICATION OF DANIEL Bourguet's books in English is a valuable contribution to the literature of contemplative theology and spirituality that will nourish and inspire the faith of all who read them. Daniel Bourguet, a French Protestant pastor and theologian of the Huguenot tradition, lives as a monk in the mountainous Cévennes region in the South of France. There at his hermitage near Saint-Jean-du-Gard, Daniel maintains a daily rhythm of prayer, worship, Scripture reading, theological reflection, and spiritual accompaniment. All of his books flow out of a life steeped in love of God, Scripture, and the seekers who come to him for spiritual support.

I first met Daniel Bourguet in 1988 when my wife, Gracie, and I moved from rural Central America to study theology at the Institut Protestant de Théologie (IPT), where he taught Old Testament. The IPT is the Église protestante unie de France's[1] denominational graduate school in Montpellier, France.

Prior to our move to France while ministering among impoverished farmers in Honduras in the 1980s, we had come across the writings of Swiss theologian Wilhelm Vischer and French theologian Daniel Lys by way of footnotes in Jacques Ellul's inspiring books. Vischer had written a three-volume work entitled *The Witness of the Old Testament to Christ*, of which only volume 1 is translated into English.[2]

1. Then the Église réformée de France.
2. Wilhelm Vischer, *The Witness of the Old Testament to Christ*, vol. 1, *The*

That book, along with a number of articles and Daniel Lys' brilliant *The Meaning of the Old Testament*,[3] exposed us to a community of Bible scholars who articulated a continuity between the Old and New Testaments that was highly relevant then and now. This connection would ultimately lead me to Bourguet.

We experienced firsthand how a literal reading of the Old Testament in isolation from the New Testament confession that Jesus is both Lord and Christ (Messiah) brings great confusion, division, and even destruction. In rural Honduras churches often distinguish themselves by selective observance of Old Testament laws and use certain Old Testament stories to inspire fear of God as punishing judge. In North America Christians were drawing from the Old Testament to justify the death penalty and US military intervention in Central America and beyond.

Wilhelm Vischer himself had been an active resister of Nazism from his Old Testament teaching post inside Germany. He resisted the misuse of Scripture to justify anti-Semitism, nationalism, and war, insisting on the importance of the Old Testament for Christian faith at a time when it was being dismissed. He was consequently one of the first professors of theology to be pressured to leave his post and eventually depart Nazi Germany before World War II, and served as Karl Barth's pastor in Basel after he too left Germany. After the war, the church in France, having been widely engaged in resistance to Nazism and deeply encouraged by Barth, invited Vischer to be the professor of Old Testament at the IPT in Montpellier.

Ellul, Vischer, Lys and other French theologians were offering deep biblical reflection that led us to look into theological study in France.[4] We wrote the IPT about their graduate program and

---

*Pentateuch*, trans. A. B. Crabtree (London: Lutterworth, 1949).

3. Daniel Lys, *The Meaning of the Old Testament* (Nashville: Abingdon, 1967).

4. We were able to study with pastor and New Testament professor Michel Bouttier, who was also trained by Vischer and published broadly, including a commentary on Ephesians and a number of collections of provocative articles. Elian Cuvillier followed Michel Bouttier and is currently Professor of New Testament at

discovered that Vischer had long since retired after training several generations of pastors. His protégée, Daniel Lys, had recently retired but was still available. In Lys's place was his doctoral student Daniel Bourguet, who also had been trained by Vischer. The IPT welcomed us with a generous scholarship and we were soon making plans to learn French and move to Montpellier.

We were eager for help to understand Scripture after being immersed in Bible studies with impoverished farmers in war-torn Honduras. Disillusioned with America after being engaged in resisting US policy in Central America, we felt drawn to reflect from a different context. We reasoned that studying in a Protestant seminary with a history of persecution in a majority Catholic context would prove valuable. We left Tierra Nueva in the hands of local Honduran leaders and moved to Montpellier two months early to study French and began classes in September 1988.

Daniel Bourguet taught us Hebrew and Old Testament in ways that made the language and text come alive. He invited students into his passion and curiosity as we pondered both familiar and difficult passages of Scripture. I remember continually being surprised at how seriously Daniel took every textual critical variant, even seemingly irrelevant ones. He masterfully invited and guided us to both scrutinize and contemplate each variant in its original language until we understood the angle from which ancient interpreters had viewed the text. Daniel modeled an honoring of distinct perspectives as we studied the history of interpretation of each passage. He sought to hold diverse perspectives together whenever possible, yet only embraced what the text actually permitted, exemplifying fine-tuned discernment that inspired us.

Daniel's thorough approach meant he would only take us through a chapter or two per semester. This meant we took entire courses on Genesis 1-2:4, on Abraham's call in Genesis 12:1-4, and on Jeremiah 31, Exodus 1-2, Psalms 1-2 and others. In each of his courses he

---

the IPT, writing many high quality books and articles.

included relevant rabbinic exegesis, New Testament use of the Old Testament, and the church fathers' interpretations. Daniel imparted his confidence that God speaks good news now as he accompanied us in our reading, making our hearts burn like those of the disciples on the road to Emmaus—and inspiring us to want to do this with others. In alignment with Vischer and Lys he demonstrated through detailed exegesis of Old Testament texts how God's most total revelation in Jesus both fulfills and explains these Scriptures, making them come alive through the Holy Spirit in our lives and diverse contexts.

While living in France every summer Gracie and I traveled from France to Honduras, spending several weeks sharing our learning with Tierra Nueva's Honduran leadership and leading Bible studies in rural villages before returning back for classes in the Fall. We had pursued studies in France with the vision of bringing the best scholarship to the service of the least in a deliberate effort to bridge the divide between the academy and the poor. Our experience of the rare blend of scholarship and pastoral sensitivity, which you will see for yourself in his books, contributed to us feeling called back to the church, into ordained ministry and back to the United States to teach and minister there. I benefited from his being my dissertation supervisor as I continued to integrate regular study into our ministry of accompanying immigrants and inmates as we launched Tierra Nueva in Washington State.

Daniel Bourguet's writings are like high-quality wine extracted from vineyards planted in challenged soil. Born in 1946 in Aumessas, a small village in the Cévennes region of France, Daniel Bourguet grew up in the heartland of Huguenot Protestantism, which issued from the Reformation in the sixteenth century. He pursued studies of theology at the IPT in Montpellier, including study in Germany, Switzerland and at the Ecole Biblique in Jerusalem. In lieu of military service, Daniel served as a teacher in Madagascar. He was ordained as a pastor in the Église réformée de France in 1972, serving parishes from 1973 to 1987. Daniel wrote his doctoral dissertation[5] while serving as

---

5. See Daniel Bourguet, *Des métaphores de Jérémie*, Paris : J. Gabalda, 1987.

a full-time parish pastor—a common practice in minority Protestant France, where teaching positions are scarce and pastors are in high demand. This practice often proves fruitful for ordinary Christians and theologians alike, deepening reflection and anchoring theologians in the church and world.

During our residential studies in Montpellier from 1988 to 1991, Gracie and I witnessed Daniel's interest in the early monastics and fathers of the Eastern church. In 1991 Daniel became prior of La Fraternité Spirituelle des Veilleurs (Spiritual Fraternity of the Watchpersons) and felt called to be a full-time monk, leaving the IPT in 1995 for a year in a Cistercian monastery in Lyon before moving to his current site in Les Cévennes in 1996.

Joy, simplicity, and mercy are the three pillars of Les Veilleurs, an association of laypeople and pastors founded by French Reformed pastor Wilfred Monod in 1923 (with a Francophone membership of 400 in 2013). Members of this fellowship commit to pursuing daily rhythms of prayer and Scripture reading, including noontime recitation of the Beatitudes, Friday meditation on the cross, regular engagement with a faith community on Sundays, and spiritual retreats and reading that benefits from universal devotional and monastic practices. Les Veilleurs has served to nourish renewal in France and influenced the founding of communities such as Taizé. Under Daniel Bourguet's leadership Les Veilleurs thrived. As a member of Les Veilleurs I attended many of his annual retreats, witnessing and experiencing the vitality of this movement firsthand.

Daniel Bourguet's teaching and writing since his departure from his professorship at the IPT in 1995 have focused primarily on equipping ordinary Christians to grow spiritually through engaging in devotional practices such as prayer, Scripture reading, and contemplation. Other works that will hopefully appear in English include reflections on asceticism, silence, daily prayer, and the Trinity. All but three of Daniel's twenty-five or so books are based on his spiritual retreats offered to pastors and retreatants with Les Veilleurs. He has offered retreats to Roman Catholic, Orthodox, and Protestant communities throughout France and Francophone Europe and is widely read and appreciated as a theologian who bridges divergent worlds and nourishes faithful Christian practice in France. Daniel Bourguet made his first and only visit to the United States in 2005, offering a spiritual retreat in Washington State. He accompanied me to Honduras on that same trip just after Hurricane Katrina ravaged the country, teaching Tierra Nueva's leaders and accompanying me as I led Bible studies and ministered in rural communities.

Daniel left his role as prior in 2012 and now continues his daily offices, receives many seekers for personal retreats, and offers occasional retreats where he lives and writes. In alignment with the early monastic commitment to manual labor, Daniel weaves black and white wool tapestries of illustrations of biblical stories done by pastor and painter Henri Lindegaard. Daniel's unique contribution includes his Trinitarian approach to biblical interpretation wherein he reads Scripture informed by the early church fathers, with special sensitivity to how texts bear witness directly but also indirectly to Jesus, the Father, and the Holy Spirit.

Daniel Bourguet models an approach to Scripture and spirituality desperately needed in our times. He reads the Bible with great confidence in God's goodness, discovering through careful reading, prayer, and contemplation insights that feed faith and inspire practice. Daniel's deliberate reading in communion with the church fathers brings the wisdom of the ages to nourish the body of Christ today. His tender love for people who come to him for spiritual support, and the larger church and world inform every page of his writing, inspiring like practice. May you find in this book refreshment, strength, and inspiration for your journey as you are drawn into deeper encounters with God.

Bob Ekblad

Mount Vernon, WA
July 7, 2016

# Preface

THIS BOOK REPRISES STUDIES given at a retreat of *La Fraternité spirituelle des Veilleurs* held at Orsay in March 2000. In retreats, as with preaching, bibliographic references are left to one side; these might have had their place in marginal notes, but I have preferred to keep them to a minimum in order to stay close to the style of a retreat, as if the reader had also been invited to take part in a retreat through this book.

The people present at these retreats were believers, Christians, and the reader will see that my remarks assume this. Nothing has been changed anything here, so a reader who is not a believer will undoubtedly feel uncomfortable at times; for the multitude of questions that will arise for such a reader I ask pardon; however, to go on a retreat is to retire from the world for a time to be face to face with God, and the teaching at a retreat is a means to that encounter; for this, a person would have to be a believer. You need to know this before starting to read the book; I am speaking here as if at a retreat, to a reader who is a believer.

Finally, again as if on a retreat, I have kept the elements of an oral style. You are addressed here as a "reader friend," in the form of a dialogue, a dialogue that doesn't propose to be more than an overture to the most sublime of dialogues, that with God.

So there we are, my reader friend! May your dialogue with God find something here to nourish it.

— CHAPTER 1 —

# Repentance—Good News

TODAY REPENTANCE IS NOT an everyday topic any more than it is fashionable to talk about sin. In our day, an awareness of sinfulness is far from being shared by all. Sin and repentance; the words are a little antiquated, and it might be thought puzzling to make them the subject of a book. It may even be, reader friend, that as you open these pages you feel a certain apprehension, wondering where it will all lead!

However, I am forcibly impressed by the number of people who are preoccupied with issues of sin, repentance, and forgiveness, yet without necessarily being able to put these great realities of life into words. Many of those who come to see me are oppressed, whether they realize it or not, whether they say so or not, by this issue, the issue of sin and repentance. Most of the time they are troubled by the shadows in their lives, weighed down by faults under which they labor; they thirst to talk about such things, and want to know how to bring it all before God. It is in great measure because of people like this that I am endeavoring to reflect on our topic of repentance; and it's in thinking of them that I pore over the Bible looking to find the words that will state things clearly.

Sin, guilt, remorse, repentance, forgiveness—these are all well and truly realities of life; how are they to be experienced before God? There is always heightened apprehension at the idea of God looking into the dark place of our hearts, particularly at those things in us which are despicable . . . How true this is! However, I would like to

1

say at the outset, with great joy, that repentance, as a gift from God, is a pathway of light, a pathway of healing and of liberation. I speak of repentance like this simply because that is how I have always seen it, primarily because this is how I understand it in the mouth of Jesus—not as a supplementary issue but as a fundamental point in our relationship with God.

I don't know if you have noticed that in Matthew's Gospel the very first publicly spoken word of Jesus is an invitation to repentance: "Repent!" he says in Matthew 4:17. The first word of his first act of preaching! This is a remarkable fact. Up to this point, when he begins to preach in Galilee, no one, in Matthew's Gospel, had previously heard him speak other than John the Baptist in a short private interview (3:14–15); no one, that is, apart from the tempter, in another astonishing encounter, to which there was no witness (4:1–11). After his baptism, after his combat with the tempter, Jesus was finally able to begin his preaching ministry, and it is then that we hear as his first word, this—"Repent!"

To show the importance of this inaugural preaching, Matthew sees fit to introduce it with a prophecy, one which is a striking setting for the issue of repentance: "The people who sat in darkness have seen a great light; and for those who sat in the land of the shadow of death, a light has arisen" (4:16).

To be sure, the light is Christ, but it is also his preaching, his invitation to repentance in the midst of the darkness of our sin. "Repent!" says Jesus. Matthew makes this appeal a burst of light breaking forth into our night. Repentance, a pathway of light! This really isn't what we are accustomed to think!

"A light has arisen": Matthew seizes on the prophetic word to illuminate this, the threshold of the gospel, the threshold of the good news to be proclaimed by Jesus. "Repent!" This is the word with which the good news begins!

"Repent!" If we wish to enter into the heart of Jesus' message and then act in concordance, it is absolutely necessary that we properly

2

understand this first invitation he speaks to us, and to respond by doing what he says. How, in fact, can we go any further if we ignore
this initial instruction? To take the gospel seriously means beginning
at the beginning and, so, putting repentance into practice. This is the
threshold we have to cross to gain entrance into the good news that is
presented to us: "Repent, because the kingdom of heaven is at hand"
(Matt 4:17).

Repentance at the threshold of the good news of the kingdom;
this is what we are to receive from the Lord!

Before Jesus ever began to preach, John the Baptist was instructed
to prepare the way for him; he too had done this by setting out to
preach. What was the Baptist's message? It's amazing. According to
Matthew, the very first public word of John the Baptist was exactly the
same as that of Jesus: "Repent" (3:2). John the Baptist and Jesus said
absolutely the same thing, and they even added to it the same expan-
sion on their invitation: "Repent, because the kingdom of heaven is at
hand" (3:2 and 4:17). The entirety of their first proclamation is exactly
the same! It is possible that there are nuances to distinguish if we are
to correctly understand what might have been intended by these words
in the mouths of the Baptist and of Christ, and we will make efforts to
examine those distinctions; but it is certainly the case that the two men
were agreed about the tight link between repentance and the coming
of the kingdom.

It may be that John the Baptist, as the forerunner to the gospel of
Christ, made repentance a preface to it, whereas, with Christ, repentance is an integral part of the gospel message. Mark specifies: "Jesus
proclaimed the Gospel of the kingdom of God,[1] saying ". . . Repent
. . ." (1:14–15) Repentance here is "the Gospel of God."

When Luke summarizes the teaching of John the Baptist he
doesn't, however, present the teaching as a preamble to the gospel, but
as an element of it. For Luke, in fact, all the Baptist's exhortations,

1. The French text says "the gospel of God," following the Segond translation.
(Translator's note)

including that of repentance, form part of the gospel. "In this way, and with many other exhortations, he proclaimed to the people the Good News" (3:18).[2] John the Baptist and Jesus, then, are very close in the way they make repentance the first word of the good news.

To grasp the nuances and differences there might be between the preaching of John and Jesus is doubly important for us Christians, firstly if we are to practice repentance according to Jesus' conception of it rather than John's, but also if we in our turn are to preach it. Jesus, indeed, instructed his disciples to preach that the kingdom of heaven has come nigh (Matt 10:7), and that this closeness is inseparable from repentance. Mark clearly notes this with regard to the disciples' first mission; "they went out and proclaimed the need to repent" (6:12).

Whose disciples are we when we preach repentance? Whose disciple, indeed, am I in speaking here of repentance—of John or of Jesus? If the Baptist and Christ expressed different content in the same words, it is absolutely essential to know precisely what that content would be; we don't wish to be led astray ourselves or to mislead those to whom we speak.

Perhaps too, and this is what we will discover, if there are differences between the Baptist and Christ in their conception of repentance, it is not that we should accept one and reject the other, but rather that we practice both as a necessary continuum. In fact Jesus himself underwent baptism as preached by John, which is to say, a baptism of repentance (Mark 1:4). Jesus never disavowed either the baptism he received or John's preaching. Some of Jesus' disciples, indeed the very first, had originally been disciples of John before following Christ (John 1:35–37). These disciples heard both teachings and must have grasped and passed on the difference. Was it a case of continuity or rupture? Repetition or innovation? Or was it rather a deepening? It seems to me we should gather from the New Testament that it is more correct to think of a deepening and strengthening from John to Jesus,

---

2. The KJV does not translate *evangelion*, "gospel," leaving it assumed in the word "preach." (Trans.)

as if there are levels of repentance and John and Jesus invite us to enter at different levels.

The Baptist's preaching is therefore not invalid. It is retained by the Evangelists, not in some kind of opposition to that of Christ, but to show the continuity between the two, their complementarity, making the one appear as a launching pad for the other. What the Baptist preaches is the gospel, as Luke specifies; what Christ preaches continues to be the gospel, but in its fullness.

"Repent," said John; "repent," Jesus improves. We receive the preaching in the order the Evangelists give it. Firstly, we engage with repentance as spoken by John the Baptist, then as spoken by Christ, and there is no stopping along the way for us, as true disciples of Christ.

## Repentance or conversion?

Before going any further, it is very important that we grasp the meaning of the biblical words.

"Repent," say John the Baptist and Jesus according to many translations[3] (Matt 3.2 and 4.17); "be converted," says the TOB; "turn around," says Chouraqui; "change your behavior" says another, these last two following more the idea of the TOB.

It is indeed "repent" that we should understand. In fact the Greek verb *métanoéo* means exactly "repent," whereas "to convert, turn" is the translation of *épistrépho*. It is quite mistaken to run the two verbs together, so I find it difficult to understand when this is done. It's true that the two verbs are very close and almost synonymous in the literature subsequent to the Bible, but we should not engage in anachronism. The New Testament is not to be explicated through later writings but in terms of the Old Testament Greek (the Septuagint) that precedes

---

3. The author refers to various French translations; English versions are more settled on "repent" than the French, but the same range may be found. (Trans.)

it, and on which it is based in a very evident way. The New Testament sees itself as the continuation of the Old.

In the Septuagint, *métanoéo* always translates the Hebrew *nâham* in the niphal form (fourteen times); this means simply "to repent" and not "be converted." For its part, *épistrépho* massively translates the Hebrew *shouv* (408 times), which means simply "to be converted" and not "to repent."

The Septuagint never translates *shouv* by *métanoéo* (with the possible exception of Isaiah 46:8, over which the Septuagint Concordance hesitates). It never translates *nâham* by *épistrépho*. We should not confuse the two where the Septuagint and New Testament don't.

Again, if Christian writers have continued to make this confusion between repentance and conversion, it is a lack of respect for the Bible and perpetuates a misunderstanding. We can tolerate Calvin being able to write in his *Institutes* that "the word the Hebrews had to signify penitence means conversion or turning";[4] but it is very difficult to accept P. Bonnard, today, explaining the Greek word *métanoéo* on the basis of the Hebrew *shouv*, when the Greek word translates *nâham* and not *shouv*.[5]

If there is no possible confusion between repentance and conversion in the Greek of the Septuagint, I can see no reason why there should be any over the Greek of the New Testament. I maintain the importance of this distinction if we are to properly understand the biblical texts.

Conversion (*shouv* or *epistrepho*) is a change in behavior and most commonly a turning towards God, with a very vivid Hebrew image of a change in direction along a road, a turning back on one's tracks for one who is far from God. The image is maintained in the Greek, since *strepho* also means "to turn back."

---

**4.** Book III, 3.5, *Institutes of the Christian Religion.*

**5.** With regard to Matthew 3:2 in his commentary on *The Gospel according to Saint Matthew,* Delachaux et Niestle, Neuchatel, 1963.

Repentance is a more internal change, at the level of thought; it is a change of sentiment or point of view.

There is plainly a link between repentance and conversion, a connection of cause and effect. Repentance comes first, and it is because there is a change in thought that there is a subsequent change of behavior. The change of sentiment leads to a change in attitude. Repentance brings conversion.

"Repent," say John the Baptist and Jesus, which is to say, begin to change within yourselves, in your heart, and that, surely, will lead to changes in the way you behave.

— CHAPTER 2 —

# On the Threshold of the Gospel

"Repent": this is the first word in the mouth of John the Baptist. We need to take in what this says and then put it into practice if we are to be really ready to then understand Christ properly and follow him.

The desert fathers understood perfectly that repentance is a first, necessary step in the Christian life. Thus, for example, Abba Gelase, discovering his inability to follow the ascetic practices, said to himself, "Since you are incapable of performing the works of the desert, stay seated patiently in your cell and weep for your sins and never leave . . ." (Sentence 181).[1]

For his part, Abba Isaie asked Abba Macarius, "Give me a word." The old man replied, "Flee men" (in saying this Abba Macarius was stating the first step to becoming a monk). Abba Isaie then asked him, "What does it mean to flee men?" The old man replied, "To sit in your cell and weep over your sins" (Sentence 480).

This was the repentance preached by the Baptist in the wilderness; an invitation to weep over one's sins before God, confessing them to him. Then the heart, liberated by God's forgiveness, becomes ready to hear the first words of Christ.

---

1. From *Sentences of the Desert Fathers.*

## The unfolding of repentance _____

We will go a little further into the details of repentance so that we can see more precisely what takes place.

The verb *métanoéo* is a composite word formed from a preposition *méta* which means "after," and a verb *noéo* which means "to think." *Métanoéo* therefore means "to reflect after some word or fact which brings an internal change."

Everything begins then with something that sets in motion a change at the level of reflection. This "something" needs to be examined. It could be something spoken that causes me to see my sin, which reveals it to me, whether I was ignorant of it, or because I intended to hide it from myself. The words would generally be those of a person, but one way or another it always eventuates in discerning, sooner or later, that through these words it is God who is speaking to me—because God is the only one who can really make me aware of my fault. Another person may be mistaken when dealing with my faults, but God is never wrong. He makes things clear through whomever he chooses to show me my sin.

Consciousness of my fault may also be effected by some event, a fact, a righteous action, a look, a picture, a silence . . . in short, through any external event that God uses to make me see.

My sin will often be revealed by my conscience. To demonstrate clearly the way our conscience is also used by God to speak to us, the Fathers generally considered it as being the voice of our guardian angel. John Climacus says it like this: "the conscience is the speech and the reproach of the guardian angel who is given us at the moment of our baptism. We understand that this is why the unbaptized don't feel as intensely in their soul the piercing of remorse for their evil actions."[2] Calvin is less assertive and contents himself with saying that the conscience is "like a witness . . . a guard who is given man to watch over and look out for him, and to uncover all that would be easy to hide

2. John Climacus, *The Ladder of Divine Ascent.*

whenever that is possible."[3] We could simply say that our conscience is that voice within which is a lively echo of the word of God.

Finally, very frequently, and this is the most important method, it is through some word from the Bible that God reveals our sin to us.

Some person, some event, the conscience . . . At the time of Christ, we see John the Baptist coming on the scene as the one God would use to help the crowds become aware of their faults. The Baptist himself saw very clearly that he was nothing more than an instrument of God, which is why he says so humbly: "As for me, I am the voice of one crying in the wilderness" (John 1:23).

A voice, and that's all! But a voice through whom God's call could be heard.

It's a voice that had to "cry" because the human heart is often deaf. Only the humble hear words that denounce their sins. The proud cannot hear this type of speech; their opinion of themselves is too high; they are too indulgent, too complacent with regard to themselves.

Not only had John the Baptist to raise his voice, but he needed to use violent words to unstop the ears blocked by pride. "You generation of vipers"; such was his invective (Matt 3:7).

This voice cried "in the wilderness," which is to say in the solitude and silence, before God, in a place where it was hard to run from God's word. In the bustle of daily life, it becomes hard to know our sins, and at times even to know ourselves sinful. In contrast, solitude before God allows us to become aware of our faults. We cannot stay long in the wilderness without seeing what God wants us to see, without understanding what we had not wished to understand. As a result of solitude, as a result of silence and the presence of the Lord, we always eventually become aware of things that otherwise it would take a long time to see. A desert ascetic explained this reality to some visitors: "He waited a moment in silence, put some water in a bowl and said to them, 'Consider this water,' and it could be seen swirling around. After a short while, he said to them again, 'Look now, how the water

3. Calvin, *Institutes of the Christian Religion,* book IV, 10.3

is still,' and when each one approached the bowl they saw their faces as if in a mirror. He said to them, 'In the same way, a person who lives among people, because of all the commotion and agitation, cannot see his sins, but when he lives alone, above all in the desert, then he sees his failings'" (Sentence 1134).

To go on a retreat, reader friend, is also a visit to the desert, and it can be a first step on the road of repentance.

## Compunction

The discovery of our sin causes us to suffer acute pain, which the Greek likens to the pain of multiple stabs to the heart; this is compunction, in Greek *katanuxis*.

This word *katanuxis* comes from a verb meaning "to puncture" and is found just once in the New Testament, in an extremely significant passage where it is used to describe the crowd in Jerusalem on the day of Pentecost; "After hearing these things, they were cut to the heart" (Acts 2:37).

The words in question were those of Peter, who had just revealed on God's behalf the peoples' great failing, that of crucifying Jesus (2:36). This revelation brought about a smarting pain to the heart, as the text specifies.

From this suffering come tears, which in such a case always flow in the heart and often down the cheeks too. We have seen the importance of repentance in the walk of the desert fathers, who speak of it with the expression "to weep over one's sins." This repentance is so great that certain ones among them spent their whole time in tears. It is thus said of Abba Arsenius that "all his life, as he sat at his manual work, he wore a cloth to catch the tears that flowed from his eyes" (Sentence 79). It is in this sense that we can understand Psalm 6, which from the outset presents itself as a psalm of repentance and develops its theme like this:

"I am worn out with my groaning; every night my eyes flood my bed, I soak my couch with tears; my eyes fail with grief" (6:6–7).

## Confession

Under the effect of this pain, the Jerusalem crowd asks Peter what attitude they should take; "what must we do?" (2:37). It's then that Peter replies, "Repent!" (2:38).

In this "repent" of Peter's, we must understand more precisely the confession of sins, the admission of guilt. An authentic confession of sins always entails tears of compunction. In fact compunction not only precedes confession but, quite equally, accompanies it.

The people as a whole take this way of repentance, but Peter specifies that the collective response rests on the personal attitude of each person; this is why he says in continuation: "Each one of you must be baptized in the name of Jesus Christ for the forgiveness of your sins" (2:38). This proposes a baptism in which each individual must confess the sin Peter denounced, as well as sins peculiarly their own.

The confession of a wrong is normally made, when this is possible, in the presence of the victim or the one who has been offended, whether this be God or humanity (see Luke 17:3–4 concerning a brother). But we need also to be aware that each time anyone is offended, God is hurt too; Jesus signals this in the parable of the prodigal son, putting into the mouth of the prodigal the following as he addresses his father: "I have sinned against heaven and against you" (Luke 15:21). That is to say, against you, my father, but also and above all "against heaven" (and heaven means here God). This is absolutely correct: from the moment we make an attack on any person, given the bond of love that exists between God and each of his creatures, it is also God we are attacking. So any movement towards repentance between people must be accompanied by a movement to repentance towards God.

The admission of guilt is made in the opening of the heart and then in the manifestation of the heart's tears. To show the heartfelt tears, the people of the Bible had the custom of enacting their repentance in the garb of mourning, which is to say, clothed in sackcloth and with ashes on the head. This explains why Jesus speaks of repentance "in sackcloth and ashes" (Matt 11:21). It is indeed mourning, since the sin brings with it a rupture in relationship such that any friendship is as good as dead.

## Asking for pardon, forgiveness, and peace

Confession is always accompanied by a request for pardon, in the tears of compunction.

When pardon is granted, this comes as a consoling comfort; the tears of compunction then disappear. By forgiving, the offended party turns consoler.

Solace, consolation, is so closely tied to repentance that the same Hebrew verb (*nâham*) means both "repent" and "console." In reality, if we look a little more closely, the consolation is twofold; by confessing his fault the penitent consoles the one he offended; and, by forgiving, the offended one consoles in turn. There is thus reconciliation and ensuing peace; and with peace we have reached the end of the process of repentance.

The reconciliation itself can be so revolutionizing that it too can bring tears to birth, though such tears are no longer the bitter tears of compunction, but the sweet and joyous tears of peace. The more profound the repentance, the deeper will be the peace and joy of reconciliation.

The peace received through God's forgiveness is often short-lived and this can be very surprising to us. This does not mean that God has given us a fragile peace! On the contrary it means that our repentance was rather superficial. Any peace received from God is real and solid, but its duration reveals the quality of our repentance. If peace becomes established in us, it is because our repentance was deep. By contrast, if the peace doesn't last, it is because our repentance was superficial. God's forgiveness is total, but repentance receives it to the degree of the repentance.

The process of repentance is of such price in God's eyes that consolation is as much a work of the Father as it is of the Son and the Holy Spirit. We are aware that Jesus gives the Holy Spirit the title of Comforter[4] (John 14:16, 26; 15:26), but we mustn't forget that the same title is also attributed to Christ in 1 John 2:1 ("we have a comforter with the Father, Jesus Christ"). When it comes to the Father, while he isn't given the title comforter, we nevertheless find he is the subject of the verb "to comfort" in a passage that shows him too in the office of comforter: "Blessed be God, the Father of our Lord Jesus Christ, the Father of mercies, the God of all comfort, who comforts us in all our afflictions, so that, by the comfort of God with which are comforted, we may comfort others . . ." (2 Cor 1:3–4). Furthermore, there is also the question in Revelation of an action of the Father's that is plainly one of comfort: "God will wipe away all tears" (7:17). He is a wonderful Father to manifest his love in this way!

To forgive and to console are ways to avoid judging; they are a refusal to condemn, and this is the attitude of the prodigal son's father, who, rather than judge, takes his son in his arms. This father, Jesus tells us, is none other than God. Fortified by this revelation about God, we welcome the first public message of Jesus as truly good news. "Repent": this invitation to repentance is extraordinary. It impels us towards taking the first step along the way to encountering the infinite grace of God. Truly, to set out on the road of repentance is to head towards an encounter with grace. How good to know!

To be more precise, looking at the matter more closely, it is not we who take the first step towards reconciliation, but God himself,

---

4. The French throughout uses the word "console"; "comfort" is more traditional in English. (Trans.)

through those he sends across our path. Through both the Baptist and Christ, it is God who takes the first step and approaches: "Repent, because the kingdom of heaven is at hand." With this invitation it is God who takes the initiative and opens up the way. The ultimate grace has already preceded us! What good news . . .

## Peter, the penitent

In a chapter on repentance, John Climacus presents Peter as the prime example of repentance (Sentence 5:1). This is an apt description and provides me the occasion to illustrate the whole process of repentance with Peter as its example.

What I am going to develop at length is stated very soberly in a few verses by Matthew; it's a story we take up at the moment when Peter denies Jesus for the third time: "Peter began to curse and to swear, 'I don't know this man!' At that moment the cock crowed, and Peter remembered the word Jesus had spoken, 'Before the cock crows you will deny me three times.' Then, after he left, he wept bitterly" (26:74–75).

In the emptiness of the night after he had denied his master three times, Peter is thrust onto the way of repentance by the crowing of the cock. This simple sound is the trigger that sets off the whole process of repentance. A cock crowing sounds so very banal, but takes on immense importance for the disciple because it awakens in him a memory that forces his sin into his consciousness: "He remembered the word Jesus had spoken to him; 'before the cock crows you will deny me three times.'"

A cock crowing; this is the event that makes Peter aware of his sin. Peter comes sharply to himself and finds himself confronted by reality; he had indeed denied his master three times. This awareness sets off in him the pain of compunction. Then, Matthew tells us, "he wept"; to show the intensity of pain, he specifies that "he wept bitterly." This adverb, "bitterly," does not have the same root as the word for compunction in Acts 2:37, but it is very close, deriving as it does from a word that also describes something that is sharp, like a thorn.

The compunction is so strong that Peter cannot contain his tears; he has just enough time to quit the courtyard and lose himself in the night: "he went out and wept bitterly." In the Bible a man never weeps in public (see, for example, Gen 42:24, 43:30). It is the night here that hides Peter's tears, and, from here on, the remainder of the process of repentance unfolds in secret. Nevertheless, Matthew chooses his words remarkably well and makes clear what he only evokes, with the reticence natural when describing a weeping man.

Peter is unable to confess his fault to the one he denied. Such a confession would have witnesses and would place his life in danger. He knows that he would be risking arrest and perhaps the same fate as Jesus. Nevertheless, where he is unable to confess his failing to Christ, he can confess it to God, without witness, in the refuge-giving night as he leaves the courtyard of the high priest. God alone sees Peter's tears, and in the tears Peter opens his heart to God. His confession consists of his tears.

One factor that allows us to say this about Peter's confession is the verb chosen by Matthew to describe the disciple's tears, "he wept." The Greek verb *klaiein* is one which belongs to the category of religious lamentation; it is the way one cries before God. "Come, let us worship and bow down and *weep* before the Lord who made us" (Ps 95.6). The verb *klaiein* contains in itself a request for pardon addressed to God; silent tears can speak to God! How true this is; God understands the language of tears! This is so much the case, that Bailly's dictionary actually gives "repent" as a meaning of *klaiein*.

Matthew leaves this well understood; everything passes in silence between Peter and God, in the silence of the night. What will happen next as to forgiveness and reconciliation? Matthew says nothing, held back no doubt by delicacy; the opening of the heart in repentance is a matter of intimacy with God. But for us, reader friend, we can go a little further with no risk of indelicacy since we are dealing not only with Peter but with all of us, in our encounter with God.

The Fathers noted with clarity something that is good to know since it helps us discern the reality of God's forgiveness. God himself is modest, of great reserve. With someone who weeps over his sin in silence, God comes to bring forgiveness in silence, discreetly, but in a way that is so real it cannot escape the attention of the penitent person. The one who weeps suddenly discovers that the bitter tears become extremely sweet. He is then amazed; how could what was so bitter become so sweet? Then the answer becomes evident; God alone is able to transform tears like this. This discreet transfiguration of the tears speaks magnificently of God's forgiveness. The sweetness of the tears contains God's pardon. The experience brings certainty; the tears being shed are those of joy and peace in the infinite goodness of reconciliation with God . . .

It s good to be able to talk like this, reader friend; there is matter here that greatly helps our understanding of how God's forgiveness can settle upon us as a certainty.

"When I consider," says John Climacus, "the nature of compunction, I am struck with amazement. How can something we call an affliction and sadness contain, hidden within itself, such joy and gladness, as wax holds honey? What lesson should we draw from this? It is that compunction of this nature needs to be recognized in a special way as a gift from the Lord. There is no longer any pleasure for the soul in what is not true pleasure; but there is a secret comfort from God for the crushed heart" (ibid., 7:54). "The groaning and sorrow cry out to the Lord; the tears caused by fear intercede in our favor; and the tears born of holy love show us that our prayer has been accepted" (7:9).

Tears of forgiveness are so beautiful and so closely tied to the grace of God that the Fathers came to liken them to a sacrament and speak of them as a "second baptism" (see Symeon the New Theologian, *Theological Chapters*). They had good reason to be so bold because, in their sweetness, the tears are charged with God's forgiveness. "Greater than baptism itself is this source of tears which gush forth following baptism, audacious though this statement might seem. Baptism, in fact, cleanses us from the sins that went before, while the tears wash away any subsequent failing" (ibid., 7:8). Our baptism cannot be repeated, but in contrast we can weep as often as we confess our sins to God.

Where Matthew is very discreet about Peter's repentance, in John we find the outcome of the process, when Christ's forgiveness is accorded his disciple. At that point, Peter knew himself to have been pardoned by God, but what about Christ? Jesus knew it was important for his disciple to be reconciled with him; he therefore orchestrates the occasion, taking the first step. Nevertheless, because this reconciliation would take place not many days after the night of denial, Jesus, full of tact, takes care not to revive the tears of compunction or to push Peter towards seeking forgiveness; it is great finesse, full of consideration on the Lord's part.

The scene is set beside the Sea of Galilee; the Risen One rejoins his disciple; a charcoal fire is lit on the shore (John 21:9): "Do you love me?" Jesus then asks (21:15). "Yes, Lord," replies Peter; but in his reply he uses a different verb for "love" (*philein*), less strong than that Christ had used (*agapân*). Peter is well aware that his love is not equal to Jesus' expectation. Peter's love is in a pitiable state, tarnished by his denial; "Yes, Lord, you know that I love you!" Peter has no need to say more; there is no need to speak of his denial; it was enough for Christ to note the change in the verb to understand; nothing in this sleight is hidden from him: "You know perfectly, Lord, the nature of my love for you!"

Jesus renews his question (21:16, again with *agapân*); and Peter renews his reply, with the same timidity in the repetition of the same modest verb, *philein*. Jesus questions his disciple a third time, just as he had been questioned three times on the night of his denial.

Jesus indeed asks, the third time, but with such kindness that he now takes up the verb used by Peter in his answers (*philein*). Lovingly, Jesus goes to the level of his disciple, not requiring more of him than he can give! In this way Jesus reconnects with one who denied him, not to crush him with shame but to lift it away. "Feed my sheep," he says to him, confirming him in the charge that had been entrusted to him, as to the other disciples, prior to the night of the denial (Matt 10:6); a charge that placed him at the side of Christ, the true shepherd (John 10:14). As a result of this confirmation, Peter now knows himself to be always loved by Christ. In the love of the Lord, forgiveness is found that is as blazing and warm as the fire lit by Jesus beside the lake.[5]

Peter is silent; it is the silence of adoration.

## Repentance and remorse

In order to understand repentance better, it would be helpful, it seems to me, to talk about remorse as well.

Remorse begins in the same way as repentance, with a word or a fact that reveals a sin and with a new awareness of this sin; the heart then undergoes a feeling of sharp pain because of the sin committed.

But then an essential difference appears; repentance turns us towards the person we have offended, to open our heart towards them in asking forgiveness. In contrast, remorse leaves the heart turned in on itself. The heart does not open up but nurses its suffering, which then increases with time; it cannot be healed, as a result of not receiving pardon. Forgiveness heals the penitent heart, but remorse is closed off to this reality.

To be remorseful means shedding tears over oneself; to repent is to weep before God.

The pain of remorse is turned solely towards the past. The fault committed belongs to the past; the suffering is present but never becomes detached and freed from the past. Remorse knows no hope.

The pain of repentance also stems from a past fault but it opens onto the future in the hope of the forgiveness and comfort that God

---

5. We might also note that in his three questions Jesus unfailingly addresses Peter as "son of Jonas." This emphasis on the word *Jonas* is perhaps a way of bringing forward the notion of grace, given that in Hebrew "Jonas" means "grace." "The son of grace"; this is Peter in Jesus' eyes. Forgiveness is to be found revealed here too, with great finesse.

may give; repentance opens onto the future, knowing that the future belongs to God.

If we go back to the account of Pentecost and the moment when the people, aware of their sin and moved to compunction, ask of Peter, "What shall we do?," the people are at the point of cleavage between remorse and repentance, the point where everything can close down and sink into remorse. Everything depends on the answer Peter gives. He could leave them in the impasse of remorse, crushed by the weight of guilt or he could should show them the way of healing, the way of forgiveness, and this is what he does: "Repent and be baptized each one of you in the name of Jesus Christ for the forgiveness of your sins" (Acts 2:37).

This moment of distinction between remorse and repentance helps us see repentance as an extraordinary piece of good news, a truly loving word, a word from God. When he says, "Repent," Peter, like John the Baptist and Jesus, becomes the bearer of God's word. Like John the Baptist, he opens the way which leads towards God, to receiving from him forgiveness and grace, reconciliation and peace, health and life.

Remorse is a path that leads us to wander through the dark land of the shadow of death. Even so, in God's grace, in this dark land there arise people of God who invite us to repentance. The good news is that remorse can turn into repentance the moment the heart opens to God to ask pardon. The heart, though shut tight in remorse, can always open in repentance. This good news, proclaimed in the darkness of remorse, is a true word of light, a signpost pointing to the way of repentance as the way of light. The good news, the word of love, the word of God, spoken by people of light; by John the Baptist, Jesus, Peter . . .

"Repent and be baptized each one of you in the name of Jesus Christ for the forgiveness of your sins and you will receive the gift of the Holy Spirit," says Peter, according Christ the place of honor.

Since the pain of compunction accompanies remorse as it does repentance, it might be better to speak of two distinct types of compunction; Paul speaks of two kinds of sorrow, "the sorrow of the world" which leads to death, and "godly sorrow" which leads via repentance to well-being, and leaves no place for remorse. Sorrow of a worldly nature is that of remorse; it leads to death if it doesn't receive the good news of repentance and grace.

"I now rejoice," writes Paul, "not because of your sorrow, but that it has led you to repentance. Your sorrow has been according to God . . . . Godly sorrow produces repentance that leads to health, and leaves no place for remorse. The world's sorrow produces death" (2 Cor 7:9–10).

To speak of godly sorrow, of godly compunction, is to say that this pain has relation to God, is open to God and to his consolation. In contrast, worldly sorrow is closed off to God and his grace.

In the same way that Peter is presented as a picture of repentance, we will find in Judas a picture of remorse.


## The remorse of Judas

"Then Judas, who had betrayed him, seeing that Jesus was condemned, was seized with remorse and returned the thirty pieces of silver to the chief priests and elders, saying, 'I have sinned in betraying innocent blood.' But they said, 'What has that to do with us! See to it yourself!' Then, throwing the money down in the sanctuary, he went away and hung himself" (Matt 27:3–5).

Just as I was astonished to see the TOB translation confuse repentance and conversion, so I was amazed to find Segond (albeit in the edition of 1910) speak of "repentance" here with regard to Judas! On this occasion the TOB, along with many others, is right to have corrected Segond on this point; *métaméléo* designates remorse, not repentance.[6]

---

6. Most of the English versions use "repent." Some reproduce what the Greek *métaméléo* seems to mean, which is "to feel sorry," "to regret." Certainly the Greek does not carry the meaning of "repent" as defined here; "remorse" is clearly the better translation. (Trans.)

All that happens to Judas is clearly presented here as remorse. He becomes aware of his sin. It isn't stated that he suffers but the account lets that be clearly understood; he finds in himself real compunction. Judas is even prepared to get out of the trap of remorse and makes an approach to the chief priests and elders, which is to say, to the representatives of God. Indeed he opens his heart, confessing his sin. He returns the price of the betrayal and thus demonstrates his desire to be rid of the weight of guilt. Judas has stepped out on the road of repentance.

Everything now depends on the response of the chief priests, on what God's representatives will say. According to their word, Judas will either advance further in repentance or sink into remorse.

"What is that to us! See to it yourself!" The word is one of rejection, and brutally closes the way of repentance, returning Judas to his remorse; it is a criminal act! Judas might even have received this word from the chief priests as being the word of God!

Judas is silent; unbearably silent! Then he withdraws, and has no refuge other than his remorse, and there he shuts himself in. He withdraws into the darkness of the land of the shadow of death! "He went away to hang himself . . . ."

I know of few texts as dramatic as this. It shows terribly the way remorse is a closure that leads to death. Indeed, remorse concludes in murder. If, as Paul says, the sorrow of the world leads to death, this sorrow is the sorrow of Judas.

What is equally scandalous in the text is what is said by the chief priests. My attention is drawn to these representatives of God because we Christians also run the risk of behaving like them. May God guard us against such words! The day of Judas's suicide is a terrible day! Nobody encouraged Judas along the way of repentance; nobody spoke to him of possible pardon; no one told him the good news of repentance . . . Lord, have pity upon us!

Reader friend, this text invites us to weigh our words when faced with the pain of those who are full of remorse; to allow ourselves to be inbreathed by the grace of God so as to be able to show the way of repentance.

Certainly, Judas had betrayed Christ, but was it not the crowd that crucified him, just as Peter proclaimed on the day of Pentecost, "you crucified Jesus" (Acts 2:36)? The whole world is implicated in Christ's death. Is there any crime more abominable than this? The crowd was cut to the heart with compunction, right to the depths. "What shall we do?" they cried. Blessed Peter for not replying to them, "What is that to me! Look to it yourselves!" but instead, "Repent." There is no word more inspired than this of Peter's, daring to draw upon the love of God, affirming that it is possible to repent of the most abominable crime. Blessed Peter, you were right; there is no sin too great to be pardoned by God!

On the cross, Christ reveals the depth of his love: "Father, forgive them, they know not what they do." The pardon requested here of God is equally for both the crowd and Judas; all were ignorant of the enormity of their actions.

"Repent!" declaimed the Baptist in the wilderness; "Repent!" repeated Christ in the dark land of the shadow of death. "Repent!" says Peter to those who crucified the Son of God. But on the day when Judas was seized with remorse, no one caused him to hear the good news of repentance . . .

Lord, have pity upon us!

Help us to understand the degree to which remorse is a road that leads to death.

Help us know how to proclaim the good news of repentance, the good news of your love that leads to forgiveness through your grace.

## To bear sin—forgiveness

To say that a sin "weighs" on us is an image, but also a very clear manner of speaking. It really is the way we feel the reality; the weight of a failing is heavy to bear, though the degree may differ.

This way of speaking is also that of the Bible. It is how Cain speaks after murdering his brother: "My fault is too heavy to bear" (Gen 4:13).

Remorse is the event of bearing your fault alone, without being able to discharge yourself of it, whereas repentance is to disburden yourself of the fault before God, in the hope that he will be able to bear the weight of the sin with us or for us; and this hope is well founded!

God himself, in fact, presents himself to his people as "the Lord, slow to anger and plenteous in kindness, who *bears* iniquity and rebellion" (Num 14:18). The verb "to bear" here should be understood in the sense of "forgive," as is done moreover by Segond, who translates here by "forgive."[7] I have retained "bear" in order to keep the image, but it does indeed speak of forgiveness.

Israel was in wonderment before such a God, and with reason! The God who thus carries the faults of his people is a God who pardons. The psalmist expresses to God his amazement: "You have shown us your love, Lord . . . . You have borne the sins of your people" (Ps 85:2–3).

The prophet Micah also states his wonder, together with his confident hope, in explicit terms which further extend the image: "To what God are you to be compared, you who bear sin . . . . Once again you will cast all the sins (of your people) into the depths of the sea" (7:18–19).

King Hezekiah also expressed his awe in similarly vivid terms: "You have cast all my sins behind your back" (Isa 38:17).

To speak of forgiveness in pictures such as this helps us grasp the particularity of how God goes about forgiving.

---

7. This is the usual translation in the English; the Hebrew means "lift, bear." (Trans.)

At times God completely removes the sin, to throw it "into the depths of the sea," or "behind his back." Then the penitent can say with the psalmist: "I confessed my sin to you; I did not hide my fault. I said, 'I will confess my offences to the Lord'; and you, you have lifted the weight of my sin" (Ps 32:5). The whole process of repentance is present here to the point of its complete fulfilment, that is, the definitive forgiveness of God, who takes the sin to himself alone in order to totally free the one who prays.

Sometimes, however, we may feel that the weight of our sin has not completely disappeared despite having been confessed to God. The weight is lightened, but a part still remains. We need to know at this time that the repentance was not in vain. God, in fact, has drawn near to us and carries the weight of the sin with us. The pardon is not yet complete, but the penitent truly has reason to marvel all the same: God is there beside him, bearing his fault with him! What wonderful proximity from God, a proximity that gives to prayer a special savor. And what a wonderful teacher too, inviting us by his closeness to speak to him further of the load he is carrying with us; then the day comes when he makes us know that he has taken the whole thing on his shoulders and cast it to the bottom of the sea! If the forgiveness is not always immediate, God, by contrast, is never tardy in drawing near to bear the sins of those who call upon him. This too is part of the good news of repentance . . .

When God takes it all upon himself, taking the weight from our shoulders, it's then that the bitter tears of compunction turn into the sweet tears of deliverance . . . Joy no one can take away and peace that passes understanding . . .

## Denying guilt

Because of a lack of discernment, it may sometimes be that we speak wrongly to a person suffering because of their sin. We have too great a tendency these days to minimize or deny the guilt of a person's suffering through sin, saying, "You're not to blame! You have not sinned!" It could be that saying this is correct; there are those who accuse themselves of sins they have not committed. In such a case it is essential to remove blame, but this is not always how things are.

When someone is really at fault, denying guilt serves no purpose at all; there is no point in denying the evidence, conjuring away the reality. The sin is there with its weight, and it would be best to say that it will always be there. In a case like this it is a waste of time to shift the blame and to make someone else, only allegedly guilty, bear the responsibility.

Acting like this may be well-intentioned, but it shows a lack of discernment and runs counter to the announcement of the good news of repentance and God's forgiveness. Rather than deny the guilt of some wrong, it is good to face the truth, accept the reality of the sin, and invite the guilty party to open their heart before God. "Yes, you have sinned! Yes, you are guilty! But it is important for you to know that your remorse can turn to repentance before God, before this God who gives his pardon freely. Open your heart to him in complete confidence and lay out before him the weight that is crushing you. In his love for you and grace, he will know how, in due time, to cast your sin into the depths of the sea . . ."

To deny wrongdoing is to refuse God the right to intervene and pardon.

## Opening the heart; trust and humility

To open one's heart admitting one's faults is not easy, as we well know!

To confess a fault to the person one has offended is to run the risk of forgiveness being withheld, the risk of rejection, of condemnation, of bitterness, of the hardness of that person's heart. In the end it all depends on the amount of love the offended party has for the offender;

any forgiveness stems from this love and, for this reason, opening the heart in an appeal for forgiveness is an appeal to the offended person's love. This sense of love has been wounded by the offense—and wounded love is not always ready to extend forgiveness. To open one's heart is therefore to believe and hope that the offended person's sense of love will be strong enough to forgive despite the wound.

Opening up like this is not easy for another reason, one not dependent on the offended party but on the offender; to open the heart is a step of humility. You have to be humble to admit your fault and ask for forgiveness, and this humility is not given to everyone.

Are things different when we are talking about opening our hearts to God? Not entirely! But where God's heart too is wounded by our sin, his love, wounded though it may be, is always strong enough to be able to pardon. Even wounded in this way, God "does not fail to forgive" (Isa 55:7). Though wounded, he is always "ready to forgive, compassionate and merciful, slow to anger and rich in kindness" (Neh 9:17).

For this reason, when we open our hearts to God there is no risk of finding him hard of heart; what is at risk is our faith. Do we have enough confidence in God, enough faith to expect his forgiveness, enough trust to admit our wrongdoing? More, are we humble enough to put entirely into his hands the reality of our wretchedness?

"Whoever believes in him receives the forgiveness of sins," we are told in Acts 10:43. "God resists the proud but gives grace to the humble," James (4:6) and Peter (1 Pet 5:5) agree in telling us, drawing on Proverbs 3:34. Faith and humility; this, from our side, is what the opening of the heart depends on. Love and infinite grace; this, within God, is the soil in which our openness grows.

## In company

Opening the heart to God sometimes takes place with a witness, perhaps with their help or counsel, and this again involves risk.

When Judas, for example, went to open his heart to the chief priests and confess his sin, he knew very well that it was not they he had offended, but God. When he admitted his sin to them it was as God's representatives, to receive something back from them, a word from God. As we have seen, the priests betrayed the confidence he placed in them. They also betrayed God, excluding him. They put up a fence between Judas and God, a barrier, by taking on themselves what belonged to God. "What is that to us? Look to it yourself!" They ignored God and marginalized themselves too; but they walled Judas into his death-dealing solitude.

Judas had a right to expect something more; not "Look to it yourself," but "Look to it, you and God together; what's gone on is between you"; not "What is that to us?," but "This is of great importance to God; your confession of sin is very important to him; this opening of your heart is of great price in his eyes! God never rejects those who trust in him."

This Gospel episode brings us up against the role another person can play in the process of repentance towards God. Their essential role is to lead the penitent towards God, and this also, it seems to me, at different stages of the process.

In contrast to the representatives of God whom Judas encountered, John the Baptist and Peter, not to mention Jesus, step forward as excellent fellow travelers on the way of repentance, and in each of their cases we can note a few important moments when another person can bring help which is far from negligible.

Firstly, at the outset of the process, at the moment of becoming aware of the sin, someone alongside can help or even provoke this sense of awareness. This is what Peter did, for example, on the day of Pentecost. The crowd had no consciousness of having crucified Jesus, but Peter's discourse is such that they are suddenly aware of their sin. Peter's words were more than a help; they straightforwardly revealed the fault and brought about the crowd's new understanding.

At this moment, had Peter not intervened again, he might have pushed the crowd into remorse. It is here that his help becomes still more vital.

By proclaiming "repent," Peter, like John the Baptist and Jesus, enabled the crowd to pass from remorse to repentance. By opening the door of repentance he enabled the hearts of these folk, rather than fold in on themselves, to open up to God.

Thirdly, Peter and John the Baptist intervene again when they propose baptism to the penitents, which is to say they indicated the means by which they could receive God's forgiveness. John the Baptist baptized "for the forgiveness of sins"; his baptism was a "baptism of repentance for the remission of sins" (Mark 1:4). As for Peter, he gave a similar invitation: "That each one of you be baptized in the name of Jesus Christ for the remission of sins" (Acts 2:38). On that day 3,000 people received baptism (2:41). Though God alone can forgive sins, it is his servants' place to proclaim this forgiveness. Jesus himself, having been authorized to grant forgiveness (Mark 2:10), then gave his disciples power to grant it too (Matt 18:18).

Lastly, we find in the case of John the Baptist that the help brought to aid repentance is not limited to this; it goes further, inviting people to live so that the forgiveness received works out into changed behavior; "Bring forth fruit worthy of repentance," the Baptist told the crowd (Luke 3:8).

This really is what establishes conversion since conversion is the change in behavior that flows from repentance. To be converted means producing the fruit that attests the reality of the repentance.

To a crowd wishing to give the concrete expression of changed behavior, John had suggestions for each one according to their situation (Luke 3:10–14). Making efforts to bear fruit after receiving God's forgiveness is putting our thankfulness to God into real action.

We see that John the Baptist and Peter, as servants of God, were exercising a truly helping ministry; thus repentance can hugely benefit from the presence of a brother, someone really sent by God to help the process. All the phases of this helping ministry have their part in the good news of repentance, forgiveness and salvation by grace.

## God at work in repentance

In exercising this ministry, it's not enough for a disciple just to prepare the way for God's intervention; he also witnesses God's participation at each step of repentance, and this is what we look at now. The disciple who accompanies a penitent does not do so in God's absence, as though God himself did not intervene until the final step of repentance. We will see that the role of God is essential; not only is he present, but he intervenes at each step in the process.

Clearly, God is active at the end of the repentance process, giving what no one else could ever give, his pardon. It is from him that the penitent hopes for pardon and it is of him that it is asked. God alone, then, can step in and forgive; this is underlined by the fact that no one other than him really knows how to forgive effectively; this emerges very clearly from the Old Testament where the only subject of the Hebrew verb *sâlah* ("to forgive") is indeed God. Yes, God alone forgives, as Jesus affirmed in the healing of the paralytic (Mark 2:7). When, as Jesus teaches, a person has authority to give forgiveness on God's behalf, such forgiveness is received as God's, not as merely human. The human forgives in God's name, but the power, the efficacy, and the truth of the forgiveness come from God, who is finally responsible.

All this is clear, but it is also clear that God does not content himself with stepping in only at the last stage of repentance. He is involved beforehand and during the process, particularly at the moment of the invitation to repent. Nobody in fact can say "repent," unless he is in God, indwelt by him, inspired by him. When John the Baptist, Jesus, and Peter invite repentance it is because these men were in God. At the end of the day, it is God himself who, through his servants, makes the appeal and it is God himself who gives power and effective force to the appeal. Without God nobody can incline another person towards God. Walking towards God in repentance means being drawn by him; to turn to God means first having been sought by him.

This is not all; God is at work in the penitent, just as he is working in the one making the appeal. "Repent": this call is a call to life, a call that snatches a person out of the pit of remorse, protecting and preserving from suicide. Only God can snatch those who dwell in the darkness of the shadow of death out of the darkness and lead them into light.

When the call to repentance is heard and a person realizes the sin in the darkness of his or her heart, it is because God is at work and because he himself has come to shine into the darkness. It is surely necessary for God to come and visit a human heart if a person is to see their sin and confess it. Without God we are incapable of it; the heart is too dark. In short, it is because God comes to scrutinize the dark corners of our heart that we become aware of our sin. The impulse of light is so hard to bear that we begin to weep bitter tears of compunction.

In the end, there is no moment of the repentance when God is not active in our heart. It is because God visits us and carries us that we are able to set out on the road of repentance. Left to ourselves we would be lost; thanks be to God, we are at every moment guided by him as he works unseen in our heart, with the infinite discretion of love.

All this seems to me wonderfully expressed in the account of Peter's repentance. At the very moment when the cock crows, which is to say at the outset of the disciple's repentance, Luke gives us a detail he is alone in providing and which shows us how discreetly God intervenes; but it is a surprisingly forceful detail : "The Lord turned and looked directly at Peter" (Luke 22:61).

In Luke, rather than the cock's crowing it is the look from Jesus that is the trigger; a silent look of such intensity that Luke, to describe it, chose a rare and particularly evocative word, *emblépein*, which means that "Jesus *looked inside* Peter," which is to say, into his heart!

This is the same look that Jesus fixed on the rich young man, which Mark then says was a look of love (Mark 10:21). Luke had no need to specify this; it is easily understood when we realize that, in Luke, Jesus is the only subject of the verb (see here and 20:17).

It is this look that brings back to Peter's mind what his master had said: "Before the cock crows you will have denied me three times." It is the look that opens Peter's heart and shows him all at once both his sin and Jesus' wounded love. Jesus' look causes the outburst of tears and impels Peter to repentance. It is this look that in its infinite kindness immediately brings the hope of forgiveness, and also promises it will be granted. It's this that continues to carry Peter as he leaves the courtyard, and that gives him, in the emptiness of the night, the strength not to fall into despair. The look of Christ is what carries us and leads the process of repentance step by step.

Jesus and God are alone in being able to look into us like this. With great finesse, at this point of his account Luke gives Jesus the name "Lord," the name which in the Greek Old Testament translates the unpronounceable name of God: "Turning round, the Lord looked directly at Peter."

We give thanks, reader friend, that from the outset to the very end of the process of repentance we are borne along by the steadfast gaze of God. The great and good news of repentance is just this; all the length of our road to repentance we are carried by the loving gaze of God; a wounded love that in its grace renounces any chastisement and offers forgiveness. It is from this gaze that we derive our love for God.

# CHAPTER 3

# The Kingdom of Heaven is at Hand

## The same preaching . . . _____

"REPENT BECAUSE THE KINGDOM of heaven is at hand," Christ proclaims (Matt 4:17). "Repent because the kingdom of heaven is at hand" had been the Baptist's message (3:2). Why would Christ repeat what had already been said? Was John's whole ministry of no value? Was the forgiveness granted through the Baptist's baptism not of God? Was it necessary to begin all over again what had taken place on the banks of the Jordan?

The forgiveness received in John's baptism is certainly God's forgiveness. Christ in no way takes back anything of what God had given beside the Jordan; the forgiveness was very real. The ministry of the Baptist is in no way disavowed by Christ; John's preaching was truly from God and, furthermore, Jesus had honored his precursor by going to be baptized by him.

Jesus' respect for John the Baptist was so great that he gave him time to fully accomplish his Jordan ministry; so much so that while John was preaching in the midst of the crowd, Jesus kept his distance, in fact going into the wilderness where he was tempted. It is not until the very end of the Baptist's ministry that Jesus begins his. Matthew states this very well: "Learning that John had been handed over, Jesus returned into Galilee" (4:12), and it is only then that he begins to preach. There was nothing precipitous in Jesus' actions; he waited for the right time.

This is all quite clear: first of all, John had to have been "handed over," thrown into prison and no longer be able to preach. Then, "learning" of this piece of news, Jesus left for Galilee to take up the preaching; until that moment he was silent, leaving the speaking to John. Jesus didn't wish to cast a shadow over his forerunner by preaching at the same time; there was no rivalry, no disowning, but great respect, indeed a respect of great humility on the part of the one who was nevertheless the greater, "more powerful," as he was recognized and proclaimed to be by the Baptist himself (Matt 3:11).

John preached repentance; then, in his turn, Jesus preaches repentance as though taking the baton from his predecessor. This is not, however all there is to it; in Jesus' preaching on repentance there is more than simply a reenactment. We notice that the tone changes and the words no longer have the same resonance, though they are in substance the same: "Repent, because the kingdom of heaven is at hand" (Matt 3:2 and 4:17).

## In different tones

John and Jesus introduce their teaching with the same phrase, but the difference in tone becomes apparent in what follows. One thing that leaps out from John the Baptist's remarks is the severity with which he speaks; the tone he adopts is frankly one of menace: "You race of vipers" is how he assails those who come out to hear him (Matt 3:7). There is a succession of threatening images: the axe is laid to the root of the trees (3:10); he has a threshing implement in his hand; he will clean out the yard and throw all the rubbish into the fire (3:12); this fire is the fire of his anger (3:7), and it will not be extinguished (3:12).

The coming kingdom is one of anger, the anger of heaven, which is to say God's anger. It is while brandishing these threats in apocalyptic style that the Baptist invites repentance: "Repent, because the kingdom of heaven is at hand." We hear him cry out his invective, the voice of one who "cries" in the wilderness (John 1:23)!

With Jesus, in Galilee, the tone changes profoundly. Jesus is surely the one John announced, but he is not come with an axe in his hand! Indeed he comes to plead with great mercy the cause of a barren fig tree; "Lord, leave it another year; I will dig around it and give it some manure. Perhaps then it will produce fruit and if not, then you can cut it down" (Luke 13:8–9).

Jesus is not presented as coming at harvest time with implements to thresh the grain, but at the season for sowing, speaking parables in which he describes himself as a sower sowing his field (Matt 13:3–23).

The kingdom Jesus announces is not one of anger but of love; Jesus speaks of it as a marriage feast (Matt 25:1–13), which gives a quite different tone to the invitation to repent! This is an invitation given without any menacing pressure but with the heat and warmth of love; apocalypse gives place to the good news; the kingdom of love has come, so get ready to welcome it!

In order to underline the change in tone, Matthew presents Jesus' preaching as light in the darkness of death. We understand from John that the approaching kingdom still leaves the threat of death hanging over those who live in darkness; but with Jesus, the approach of the kingdom snatches from death those who had been in its power.

## It is at hand

If we want to understand the change in tone better, we need to grasp the full meaning of the phrase "is at hand"[1] as found in Jesus' mouth.

The expression "the kingdom of heaven" is clear enough. In the Jewish tradition, in order to avoid pronouncing the name of God, it was normal to replace it with other words, particularly by speaking of

---

1. The word in the French is *s'approcher*, literally "to approach, draw near"; "the kingdom draws near." (Trans.)

"heaven." This was a tradition to which Jesus was faithful. With regard to the word translated as "kingdom" (*basiléia*), it means "kingdom," "reign," and "royalty," so "the kingdom of God is at hand" also means "the reign of God is at hand" and even "God as king is at hand." But what exactly is in view with this phrase "at hand, draws near"?

The verb "draw near" is a word to do with spatial location. Thus, we read that Jesus and the crowd "drew near [or approached] Jerusalem" (Matt 21.1). What then do we make of a kingdom that "draws near."

For Israel, the royal status of God was a reality that concerned the entire cosmos; he was king of heaven, to be sure, but also the whole earth; not only does God reign over his own people but over all others too, as the psalmist proclaims: "The Lord reigns over the nations" (47:9). This reality cannot either advance or draw back spatially. No doubt the nations do not all recognize the royalty of God, but this does not prevent God from reigning over them. Since his kingdom knows no boundary, how could it extend further and "draw near" as if gaining territory?

To grasp the spatial meaning of the verb "draw near," I believe that for John the Baptist the approach of the kingdom corresponds to the approach of Christ; he is more than its representative, he is actually the king. It is because Jesus draws near that the kingdom draws near. It seems to me that this is the spatial sense of John's affirmation that "the kingdom of heaven is at hand"—it is at hand, drawing near, in the person of its king, Christ. In Jesus' mouth this spatial meaning continues, allowing us to understand the invitation like this: "The kingdom of heaven is at hand in the fact that I have come to you."

To this spatial sense we should also add a temporal meaning, which also belongs to the verb "draw near"; we see this, for example, where it says, "Behold, the hour draws near" (Matt 26:45).

Israel knew that the reign of God is a reality yesterday, today, and tomorrow; in this sense the reign of God could not become any closer today than it was yesterday. When the psalmist acclaims the reality of the reign of God in human history, he uses what grammarians call "the completed" tense, which is to say the tense which takes in all times: "The Lord reigns" (Ps 47:9, 93:1, 96:10, 97:1, 99:1) means "he reigns today, as he reigned yesterday and as he will reign again tomorrow." When the psalmist employs the "incomplete" it is in order to add a precision that removes any doubt: "The Lord will reign for ever" (146:10).

When John the Baptist announces that the reign of God is at hand in terms of time, this means that Christ has drawn near compared to yesterday and is here now: "the kingdom of God draws near in the fact that its king is coming close, in our time; he is here, in the now."

When it comes to Jesus, I believe he simply confirms what the Baptist had said, such that we understand the following: "the kingdom of heaven is at hand, because I, the king, I am here, today, speaking to you."

The close connection that unites the kingdom with its king becomes very clear in, for example, two parallel verses in Luke and Mark; where Luke writes "the kingdom of God is nigh" (21:31), Mark writes, "the Son of Man is nigh"(13:29).[2] We see that the two expressions are equivalent, as is surely correct: the kingdom is present in the Son of Man, which is to say, in the one to whom God has committed the kingdom (cf. Dan 7:13, the verse which is the main reference for "the Son of Man"). Indeed, the kingdom of heaven in the person of its king had never been so close as at the moment of the Baptist's preaching, and became still more so when Christ spoke.

The same thing is still happening for us today, each time Christ draws near to us, in prayer, in the sacraments, listening to the word, in the person of a neighbor who offers us love . . . For us too the kingdom is at hand in Christ, and he continues to draw near.

This is what we can understand from John, but, it seems to me, he does not go beyond these spatial-temporal and spiritual meanings of

2. Verse 29 does not say this in the English translations but does in the Segond French translation. (Trans.)

the verb "to draw near." I believe though that things are different when it comes to what Jesus says, since he adds another meaning, which we must now examine.

## He has come nigh

Bailly's Greek dictionary gives the verb *engizein* (to draw near) still another meaning, an emotional one: "to come close,"[3] which is to say become more familiar, more intimate. It therefore speaks of a heartfelt closeness. The same sense exists in English; I might say that I feel closer to Paul than I do to Napoleon, though this is not true in terms either of time or space. The closeness here is an emotional, spiritual matter, a question of affinity.

This meaning of the Greek word is also present in the biblical Greek, in the Old as well as the New Testament. When the psalmist, for example, complains, "My close friends are far from me" (38:11), he is speaking of his friends, his intimates and we note the contrast between "close" and "far." The distance the psalmist complains of is less geographical than it is one of behavior: they are "far," meaning less interested in demonstrating love.

Paul too employs this word to speak to the Ephesians about their closeness to God; you were far from God, he tells them, but now you are become close; you were strangers but you have become members of the family (Eph 2:13, 17). All this puts us on a relational level, to do with emotional closeness. Furthermore, to explain the change in relationship, Paul specifies that it is not the result of the Ephesians drawing near to God, but of the fact that God has taken the initiative to draw near to them. God, of himself, has become closer to them, more intimate.

---

3. The French for "draw near" is *s'approcher*; the word for "close" or "near" is *proche*. (Trans.)

When he speaks like this, Paul is perfectly in line with Christ; it is exactly what we understand when Jesus says, "the kingdom of heaven is at hand," that is, the kingdom, in the very person of God, has become a more intimate reality. God himself has taken the initiative to draw closer.

The psalmist had already said: "God is near to the broken hearted" (34:18); "he is close to those who call upon him" (145:18). This closeness of heart, this love, is not to be heard in what the Baptist says with its severity and menaces. By contrast, it is clearly there in the mouth of Jesus and in his message of love as a whole; God is making himself much closer, more intimate! This, in fact, is his good news.

This doesn't mean that God loved less yesterday than today, because his infinite love is always the same, which is to say, without measure; what it does mean is that he is now allowing a little more of the immensity of his love to be seen and revealed. For him, coming closer does not mean loving more, but manifesting, revealing it a little more.

"The kingdom of God is come closer, more intimate"; where Jesus allows himself to say what John hadn't, it is because on the day of his baptism Jesus heard what no other person had heard before. "Here is my *servant* in whom I am well pleased" was what the prophet heard (Isa 42:1); "Here is my *Son* in whom I am well pleased," Christ had now heard (Matt 3.17). The change from "servant" to "son" shows the much greater proximity of God. "You are my son," David understood (Ps 2:7); "you are my well-beloved son," Christ now understood (Mark 1:11). When God speaks like this, it is clearly a sign that he is coming much closer.

What Christ heard at his baptism for himself he begins to proclaim and share with all, with all the love with which he knew himself to be loved. "That the love with which you have loved me may be in them," he asks of the Father for all his disciples (John 17:26). Christ had already welcomed onto his bosom the well-beloved disciple (John 13:23), as he himself is the Son in the bosom of the Father (John 1:18).

The perfect intimacy between the Father and the Son is what the Son now proclaims to people, to enable them to share it too.

Abraham is known for having been a "friend of God" (Jas 2:23); the same is said of Moses, with whom God talked "as a friend talks to his friend" (Exod 33:11). This beautiful intimacy with God in the Old Testament was nevertheless reserved for a few exceptional and very rare people. But now, in Galilee, which was a semi-pagan area, Jesus begins to proclaim that God wishes to become much closer to all the subjects of his kingdom. Is there any greater good news than this? Intimacy with the King! Intimacy with God!

This increasing closeness of God is at the heart of Jesus' message, as, for example, is shown across the range of his parables. We do find, initially, that God is described as a distant king (Luke 19:12–27); but then also as a master who is close to his servants (Matt 20:1–16), and finally as a father who throws himself on the neck of his son, as we see in the parable of the Prodigal Son (Luke 15:20). The prodigal welcomed in this way by his father is not Abraham, Moses or some other particular friend of God, but each one of us. Furthermore, when the son is welcomed like this it is at the moment when he is beating the track of repentance towards his father; this parable admirably reveals how intimacy with God is proposed for us as penitents.

When speaking of God, Jesus never ceased to call him "my Father"; but neither did he ever stop referring to him as "your Father." He prays to the Father, and it is to "our Father" that he teaches us to address our prayers. A loving Father, it seems to me, is the principal face of God that Jesus reveals to us. When, as well as being our Lord, our King, our Master, God also reveals himself as our Father, it is indeed that he is making himself closer, more intimate.

In short, where there is the spatial-temporal meaning in the verb "draw near" as spoken by John, the same meaning is just as perceptible in the mouth of Jesus, but, over and above that meaning, and rather deeper, we find in what Jesus says the emotional content of the word. How then are we to enter into the depth of the word as spoken by Jesus and experience it? Only by the Holy Spirit. The Spirit indeed sounds the depths of God's heart and allows us to enter where the same love is found, that is, into the depths of what the Son has to say. The Spirit alone can enable us to enter into the intimacy of the Father and the Son since he shares in it, in the love of the Trinity. Compared to this, John the Baptist is perforce secondary. Only Christ, which is to say only the Son, because he is God, can say what is going on in God's heart; and only the Spirit, because he is God, can prepare our heart to open up to the divine intimacy offered to humanity. It requires the Son and the Spirit to lead us into intimacy with the Father.

"Abba," says Jesus to his Father, in a hitherto unknown intimacy. "Abba," the Spirit leads us too to say, causing us to enter into the intimacy of the Trinity (Rom 8:15).

## Drawing near is what he does

There is no one closer to us than God and yet he only approaches to a slight degree! The fact that he draws near at all allows us to hope that he will do so a little more. Why then does he not draw still nearer now? Why must we still wait? Why do we still have to pray to the Father and say, "Thy kingdom come"? There are many reasons which combine to make this so.

If he does not draw closer it is out of respect for our liberty. The kingdom of God has no limit other than our refusal, what we impose on him by the closing of our hearts, a limit God has no wish to force. Love is not true if it imposes itself with authority and fails to respect the liberty of the other. God does respect our liberty; this is why he draws no nearer. He is waiting! He awaits our yes, our *fiat*; he is waiting for us to approach him. God takes the first step and is awaiting our response before he makes a second. This is how we can understand James's statement, "draw near to God and he will draw near to you" (4:8). There is no bargaining in these words; love does not bargain.

Instead, there is a loving invitation to come closer to the one who has already drawn near to us and hopes to come closer still.

If God does not approach more nearly, it is also out of modesty.[4] Intimacy always approaches with great care; it proposes itself with reserve, without rushing the other. When we offer friendship, it is always with restraint. When he opens his heart to us a little, God invites us to do the same. He is looking for a sign of friendship in return, and that, in friendship, we will also open our hearts a little to him. If, then, in response to God's friendship, we open our hearts up to him, what kind of heart is God going to find? One unworthy of him no doubt; a pitiable heart in which sin has left deep imprints; a heart that is incapable of loving in return this God who has already opened his. If God draws near to us with great care and then comes no further, it is out of regard for us, so that we not be overcome by shame. This delicate reserve endeavors to protect the other; God does not draw any nearer because he knows what is in our heart. If he were to come too close, we would die of shame. So, in his grace, Jesus anticipates us and suggests with love, "repent"; start to prepare yourselves, before God comes any closer.

When God comes no closer it is to leave us time to prepare, time for cleansing, time for repentance, the time to be in some measure ready to welcome the Holy without compromising the intimacy he proposes, time to get on God's wavelength, holy as he is holy, perfect as he is perfect, loving as he is loving and humble as he is humble. Is there any God more humble than the one who thus approaches us, sinners? Is there a God more loving than the one who does not approach too close, leaving us time for repentance? So Jesus says to us: now is the time of repentance; therefore take time to repent! Why do you delay in repenting? Why delay, O sons and daughters of men and women? It is Love who stands at the door of your heart and knocks . . .

When God comes no closer, it is again to allow time for us to assimilate the love we find in him; this love is so great, so deep, that it is impossible for us to measure from one day to the next. There is no

---

4. The French here is *pudeur*, "modesty, reserve, delicacy." (Trans.)

doubt that we will never have enough of this life to discover all the facets of the love of God. God's love never finishes turning us upside down and doing away with every false idea we might have of him; this too lies at the source of repentance.

To repent, as we have seen, means changing the way we look at ourselves following some word which touches us and reveals our sin; this is what we hear in the mouth of John the Baptist. With Jesus things are altogether different; the word that impels us towards repentance is not the revelation of our sin but the revelation of God's love and his thirst for intimacy. The word of Christ doesn't so much invite us to change our view of ourselves as to change the way we see God. Jesus shows us God's heart, and it is faced with this revelation that we are drawn to repentance. God's love is so great that we are shaken to the depths of our beings; so great that tears of compunction start from our eyes. Our great pain is to discover ourselves incapable of loving such a God back.

In substance, the Baptist was saying, "Repent because the darkness of your sin is so great," drawing attention to our wretchedness. "Repent, because the light of his love is so wonderful," is what Christ is now saying, focusing our gaze on the infinite love of God. The Baptist was inviting us to open our hearts; Christ announces that God is opening his. Our darkness appears here too, but not in the same way; not because it is denounced but in contrast with the light. The greater this light, the more we perceive the importance of our sins; it is then that we begin to weep for sorrow.

The tears of compunction excited by Christ's message are the tears that Peter shed because of that look from him; in the discovery of Christ's infinite love Peter realizes the enormity of his denial. The greater God's love appears to us, the deeper seems our sin. In his grace, therefore, God's approach is slight. Were he to come much closer, our hearts would be unable to bear it.

## He draws near in Christ _____

To bring us an understanding of what he says about God, Jesus comes to live with us. There is nothing better he could do to reveal God's love; the face of Christ is the face of God; the love of Christ is the love of God. When Jesus draws near to us, it is God who draws near and then reveals to us, simply by drawing near, how little capable we are of returning his love.

On the occasion of his first meeting with Christ, Peter had not taken a single fish in the entire night; Jesus draws near and enables him to catch more fish than he could ever have hoped. Faced with this miracle that brings him to the discovery of an infinite love, Peter has difficulty coping with Christ being so close; he falls to his knees and pleads, "Lord, depart from me, for I am a sinner" (Luke 5:8).

A few years later, the same Peter on the night of his denial, is unable to bear so much as a look from Christ. Now, rather than beg Jesus to depart, it is Peter who departs into the night to weep.

In truth we are not ready to see God draw near to us. This is why, to prepare us, Jesus begins his very first sermon with an invitation to repent: "Repent for the kingdom of God is at hand."

Repentance, this is what we need to rediscover, not because our sin is denounced but because the love of God is revealed. If repentance prepares us to love God then it is no longer a duty imposed on us or a ritual requirement which we accomplish with more or less reticence; rather it awakens an intense desire to be put into full practice without further delay, in the hope of at last being able to love God as he wishes: "with all our heart, with all our soul and all our strength." This is the good news of the love of God, God who makes us thirst to respond to Christ's invitation: "Repent, for the kingdom of God is at hand."

— CHAPTER 4 —

# The Depth of Repentance

"REPENT BECAUSE THE KINGDOM of heaven is at hand": in the mouth of the Baptist the phrase sounds as follows, "Repent because you are sinners"; with Jesus the same phrase says, "Repent, because God is love." In the Baptist's mouth we hear "repent because the anger of God is at hand," but from Jesus, "repent because the God of love is drawing near."

Repentance is triggered by a word that reveals something. With the Baptist it was a word about ourselves, a word revealing unknown or dissembled sin; with Jesus it is a word about God, a word revealing his love, the growing proximity of which was unknown to us or perhaps concealed.

So, if repentance is a change in our point of view, with Jesus it concerns a change in our view of God rather than of ourselves. God no longer appears to us as an angry king but as a friend who wishes for greater intimacy. This discovery about God provokes in response a new awareness of the reality of ourselves. We make the bitter discovery of our own poor love and an intense thirst to be in tune with the love of God and respond to it. Our wretchedness is so great that we gauge our inability to do this, and suffer profoundly because of it; the tears of a new compunction now fill us.

We see, reader friend, that repentance is an awakening to our condition and the pain this entails, but in another way now, which is why I speak of a "new" compunction. Our wretchedness becomes apparent, but from another angle; not because it is denounced with the threat of chastisement, but because it contrasts to the highest degree with the reality of God. The contrast between the grandeur of God's love and the smallness of ours is so great that our heart begins to suffer an extreme compunction. The tears we shed are as bitter as our love for God is poor; with these tears, however, more or less of a certain sweetness always mingles itself; the one who approaches us is a being of infinite love.

What becomes apparent in us when faced with God's infinite love is not so much the detail of our sins, but the fact of our being sinful. In reality it is both, and this becomes apparent with an intensity we had not felt before. The closer God comes in his love, the more intense and deep becomes the repentance, and this is what we need to examine now. John's invitation is not obsolete, but it does now appear as a step along the road on which Jesus will conduct us infinitely further.

The closer God comes, the greater our repentance; this is a sort of axiom of the spiritual life, repeated many times over by the Fathers. To illustrate this truth they propose and develop an image that I find particularly illuminating, that of a fire heating and melting metal, leaving behind the dross. The more intense the fire, the more the metal separates from the dross as it, so to speak, becomes part of the fire itself. More precisely, it is not that the metal is purified as if it were doing the work of purification itself; no, the metal is purified by the fire. The purification is a result of the fire, not of the metal. Likewise, our repentance is a desire for purification by the intense fire of God's love. The closer God comes, the greater is the fire of his love in us, the more our sins become apparent and the deeper becomes our repentance.

A very beautiful illustration of this spiritual truth is given in the prophet Isaiah's account of his calling. "In the year King Hezekiah died, I saw the Lord seated on a throne high and lifted up, and the train of his robe filled the temple. Above the throne stood the seraphim, having six wings; with two they covered their faces, with two they covered their feet, and with two they flew. They cried one to another saying,

THE DEPTH OF REPENTANCE

'Holy, holy, holy is the Lord of Hosts! All the earth is full of his glory!' The doors were shaken in their foundations by the voice which resounded and the temple was filled with smoke. Then I said, 'Woe is me! I am lost because I am a man of unclean lips, and I dwell in the midst of a people of unclean lips, and my eyes have seen the King, the Lord of Hosts.' But one of the seraphim flew towards me, having in his hand a burning coal which he had taken from the altar with a pair of tongs. With it he touched my mouth and said, 'This has touched your lips; your iniquity is taken away and your sin is purged'" (6:1–7).

This speaks of a revelation of God in his glory and holiness. The word *love* is not mentioned, but it is contained within the very name of God, who is love. The passage is a revelation of the grandeur and holiness of God's love. The approach of such love has power to shake a man to the depths of his being, just as here the foundations of the doors to the Jerusalem temple were shaken.

The seraphim, according to the etymology of their name (*sâraph* in Hebrew means "to burn"), are beings of fire since they are close to God, whose love is a fire; and it is from this fire that a seraphim takes a simple coal, which is enough, at the end of the tongs, to purify poor Isaiah. What would have happened had these beings of fire themselves touched the man? Or if God himself had touched him? Assuredly it is God's consideration for Isaiah that means his approach was not overwhelmingly close but restrained; he draws near in love, but the degree is not great, having regard for the man, out of love for him. Before he draws yet nearer, man's place is to prepare himself by repentance. "Repent," says Jesus, "because the King is at hand," and it is in the presence of the King that Isaiah finds himself and cries out: "Woe is me . . . my eyes have seen the King."

"My eyes have seen the King," says Isaiah, though he had seen no more than the train of his robe, which in itself filled the temple! "My eyes have seen the King," though the temple was full of smoke. What would he say if he had seen more than the skirts of God's garments in the obscurity of smoke; what if he saw him face to face?

47

When he went into the temple in Jerusalem that day, Isaiah was already cleansed according to the ritual prescriptions of the time. He would not have entered had he not been thus purified. Before God, however, this purified man cries out, "Woe is me! I am a man of unclean lips and I live in the midst of a people of unclean lips!"

This is it; the closer God comes, the more our impurity appears, and the greater and deeper becomes our repentance. Here Isaiah, however ritually clean, finds in himself, with the approach of God, a double impurity, his own and that of his people; he finds that this impurity is bound to him and confesses it at once as both personal and collective, his in this second sense because of his oneness with the people.

This outlines the course we will follow as we go further into the reality of repentance. For reasons of clarity we will proceed by enumerating the levels of repentance, knowing that in experience they are intermingled. The order will attempt to correspond to the greater and greater depth of what takes place in us as God draws closer and closer.

Isaiah mentions his own impurity first, then that of his people. We will do as he did, bearing in mind the way we become aware of our own sins first; then later the collective sins become evident.

## Personal sins

If God were to cause us to see in one moment all the darkness there is in our hearts we would be totally discouraged; repentance would appear disproportionate to our actual ability and we would give up. In his kindness, God draws near slowly, at each one's pace, in step with our growth in sanctification. It is little by little that we discover the depth of our darkness and the degree to which each of our passions and vices has hidden ramifications.

Take for example our avarice, our thirst to possess, above all when it comes to money and other material goods. There is plenty enough to be done in this area of our progress into repentance. Then, as we draw nearer to God, we perceive that the thirst to possess also exists when it comes to spiritual things; we desire more gifts, more spiritual benefits, not for the edification of the church but for our own satisfaction. The awakening of our conscience to matters such as this does not take place in the blink of an eye; but the closer God comes, the more we discover in ourselves the extent of this failing, this passion.

The same could be said about appetite, greed. Beyond simple greed we find a greed for spiritual gifts and divine favor, which we hunger and thirst after for our own pleasure.

We all know how the love of power constantly seeks to ensnare us; we accept as best we can the renunciation of outward power, only to then discover the same taste for power in our behavior towards our church or in our own family. Our love of power even becomes a burden to those closest to us, those who we nevertheless love us the most!

Many more examples could be given, but I will limit myself to one final one. "A brother was a monk in a monastery, but all too often he became angry, so he said to himself, 'I will retire entirely from people; by not having to do with anyone else this passion will leave me.' So he left and lived alone in a cave. One day, after filling a jar of water he put it on the ground where it tipped over and the water spilt. He filled it again and it tipped over again. He again filled it and for the third time it tipped over. Overcome by anger, he grabbed hold of it and smashed it . . ." (Sentence 1201). In this way, alone in the desert, God showed this brother how deeply anger had established its home within.

These examples show the depth of our darkness as it appears to God. The closer God comes, the more abundant are the tears of compunction. Blessed Abba Arsenius! He must have been very close to God, never to be separated from his handkerchief! Blessed Arsenius, because God himself comforted him.

## Unconscious faults

"Forgive, O Lord, my hidden faults" (Ps 19:12).

As I pray this way, I do so knowing, as does the psalmist, that as well as conscious faults there are unconscious ones too, those that God has not yet revealed to me and that are nevertheless there in the darkness of my heart. I don't see them, but God does and I know that when he comes a little closer his light will reveal them to me. The psalmist actually takes the initiative. His thirst for closeness with God is so great that, even before God shows them to him, he asks pardon for faults he is unaware of.

God sees before we do what we don't see yet. This was the case on the night of Peter's denial when Jesus turned to look at him. Jesus, the Lord, knew that Peter had already denied him. He looked into Peter's heart, and it was only then that Peter discovered what was previously hidden.

In his grace, God chooses the moment to turn towards us, drawing near to us with just a look in order to reveal to us this or that unconscious fault. Perhaps he will wait until the last day, when we are face to face, to reveal still more woes hidden within us.

## Sins of omission

It is only on the last day that still other faults will be revealed, sins of omission, in addition to those that are known and unknown. Sins of omission are well set forth in this parable of the last day: "'Depart from me you cursed ones,' the king will say; 'be cast into the eternal fire which was prepared for the devil and his angels. I was hungry and you gave me nothing to eat; I was thirsty and you gave me nothing to drink; I was a stranger and you did not take me in; I was naked and you didn't clothe me, sick and in prison but you never visited.' Then they will reply, 'Lord, when did we see you hungry or thirsty, a stranger or naked, sick or in prison, and failed to help you?' And he will reply, 'I tell you in truth that every time you did not do these things to one of these little ones, you did not do it to me'" (Matt 25: 41–45).

This list of sins of omission is very striking. The threat hangs in the air, but in his grace Christ clarifies the parable beforehand, exhorting us to change our behavior as of today; he shines his light into our hearts, inviting us to repent: "Do you want to know why I draw no closer to you?" says the Lord. "Listen and then answer; how many times have I come close to you in the person of the hungry, the prisoner, the sick or the stranger? And you have done nothing. Repent now! There is still time! Weep with compunction! Weep over your cramped and limited love, over your heart too narrow to contain the God who draws near! How many times have I stood in tears at the door of your heart . . . ?"

Have pity on me, Lord, and in your grace be willing to forgive me; help me also to know how to love you by loving the least of your brothers. Come and animate my malingering love; where my heart is so narrow, create in me a heart meant for you. O Lord, have pity.

We will conclude here what might become far too long a catalogue of personal failings, and turn to other sins that are of equal concern.

## Collective sins

"Woe is me!" Isaiah cries out before God, in recognition of his own impurity; then he adds, "I live in the midst of a people of unclean lips," acknowledging the impurity of the people to whom he belongs.

Alongside personal sins there are the collective sins, the responsibility for which lies not with some one person but with the whole group or family, town, clan, nation . . . . The sin of a group is not the sum of the sins of each group member but another sin altogether, that committed by the group as a whole. A very good example of this is given in the Bible in the case of Sodom (Gen 19).

When the two messengers from God arrive in Sodom and receive Lot's hospitality, no particular individual takes responsibility for sinning against them. The biblical account is very clear on this point and insists on the collective aspect with very explicit, redundant over-statement: "The people[1] of the city, the men of Sodom surrounded the house, from the youngest to the oldest; the whole population without exception" (19:4). "The people of the city, the men of Sodom"; the re-statement is reemphasized with the statement "from the youngest to the oldest," and to finally really hammer home the nail, "all the population without exception"! It could not be more explicit about the collective nature of the proposed abuse.

The content of this passage is very clear. There are in fact collective abuses which no person could commit alone, without the dynamic which the whole group brings. Here it is the whole city which is guilty.

When Abraham prayed for Sodom (Gen 18:23–33) he limited himself to a particular tally of individuals, trying to ascertain how many just people were among the sinners, as though the sin were a deed of individuals alone. The continuation of the account shows that the reality is more complex, that a sin may also be collective, given that there may be a solidarity in the sin; wars show this very well! Who was responsible for the bombing of Hiroshima? The pilot? The president of the USA? The inventor of the bomb? It was an entire nation, no doubt, caught up in the collective system of evil . . .

Who is able to discern in their own hearts not just their personal sins but also the numerous bonds of solidarity that mean that the traces of so many collective sins are to be found there too? Only the intense light of God enables us to see this deep. Isaiah, in the temple, with God so close, painfully discovers all that he had never before seen in himself: "Woe is me . . . !"

In Psalm 130, we discover in the author a man as clear-sighted as was Isaiah, no doubt because God had drawn similarly close to him. When this man cries to God "out of the depths" (130:1), his cry is

---

1. The Hebrew does not specify gender but the Greek says "men."

pulled out of him by the whole assemblage of sins he confesses to God (130:3–5). At the end of the prayer we learn that these sins are "all the sins of Israel"! (130:8). There's no doubt that this man must have been particularly close to God and his light to so focus on the connections and solidarity with sin to be found in the hidden corners of his heart. The psalmist's cry is in accordance with what he sees; nevertheless, God, once again, bears this man up so he doesn't sink into discouragement; the psalmist still speaks of God's grace (130:7) with such hope (130:5) that he seeks to share this hope with the whole nation (130:7). Bless God for giving us people of such comprehension, and for carrying them, even to the depths of the abyss.

## Collective sins of ignorance

Everything that exists at a personal level also exists at a collective level. We haven't spoken of personal sin committed through ignorance because I didn't wish to make an inventory or catalogue (but see Lev 5:15–19); however we can at this point look at a remarkable example of collective sin as a result of ignorance, given us in the book of Acts.

After the healing of an invalid in Jerusalem, Peter makes a speech to the people in which he denounces a sin of this type, the murder of Jesus. In order to emphasize the collective nature of the sin, Peter speaks of the responsible parties as plural, a plural which designates the people as a whole. We see that, as he describes the different acts that led to Christ's death, Peter places the weight of what this or that person did individually on the people together. In this way he makes the people bear the responsibility for having "handed over" Jesus (Luke 3:13), when it was Judas rather than anyone else who had done this (Luke 22:4, 6, 21, 22 ,48). Peter adds that the people had "denied" Jesus (3:13), whereas he knew all too well that he alone had really denied him! (In all the accounts of the passion, Peter is the only subject of this verb.) But Peter was right! The death of Christ was not the deed of this or that individual, but was collective, the deed of all; this is why he could conclude, without mincing his words: "You killed him" (3:15).

After denouncing the murder, the collective wrongdoing, Peter specifies that the people did it "ignorantly," using the appropriate term (*agnoia*) to qualify the sin as accidental or involuntary (see Lev 5:18).

What was to be done faced with the reality of this collective sin? Peter concludes as he had on the day of Pentecost, after denouncing the same crime: "Repent!" (3:19).

Who was it who killed Christ? The Jews? The Romans? It serves no purpose to seek to apportion the blame since we are all collectively responsible for this death. We have all handed him over, denied him, killed him, though in ignorance, it is true. When God draws near to us, our responsibility appears right before our eyes. We can then turn to him in bitter tears of repentance and open our hearts to him. It's then that our bitter tears of repentance suddenly become very sweet, when we hear from the very mouth of the crucified one: "Father, forgive them, they know not what they do . . ." Infinite love! Love deeper than the deep, dark abyss of our heart!

## Turning back to the Old Testament

The collective dimension of sin had been perceived by Israel in a wonderful way, with a lucidity received from God. Nevertheless, we may note that this lucidity never went beyond the ability to see the sins of the nation, the sins of Israel. Isaiah is aware of himself as a member of a people of unclean lips. The psalmist who cries out of the depths speaks of the sins of the same nation. No one ever goes beyond, to confess the sins of mankind as a whole.

The ritual laws of the Pentateuch show that Israel was perfectly clear about collective sins. As well as sacrifices for personal sins (Lev 4:22, 27 . . . ) there were sacrifices for collective sins (4:13 . . . ). These collective sins, however, never went further than the sins of the people of Israel (4:13). There was no sacrifice for sin on a bigger scale.

On the day of Yom Kippur, the special day of repentance (Lev 16), the chief priest confessed the sins of the nation, all the sins of the nation, but nothing more. A male goat was offered in sacrifice for the sins of Israel (16:15); another goat carried the sins away with it into the wilderness, where it was chased to disburden the nation (16:21).

Nowhere in the Old Testament is there any question of confessing the sins of mankind. Where Adam and Eve had sinned, neither of them confessed their fault. Through them it is mankind that has sinned, but no one after them confessed the original failing, not Abraham, not Moses, not David, no one; and neither is there any ritual indicated for it. Repentance failed to go so far, no doubt because no one was close enough to God to see that deeply into the human heart. There is indeed, in Isaiah 53, the issue of the suffering servant who bears the sins of others, but here again the sins borne by the servant are those of the people of Israel, as the author of the text says, specifying that the servant is "stricken for the sins of *my* people" (53:8).

Then, along comes John the Baptist . . .

## The conversion of John the Baptist _____

John was a man of his own people, fashioned by the Scriptures. Those who came to hear him and to be baptized by him all belonged to the same nation. The Baptist's horizon was that of Israel.

But then, after baptizing Jesus, John no longer speaks in the same way. The tone and the import of what he says changes radically. Until then, John had spoken of the one to come, underlining his power (Matt 3:11); after baptizing him, he points to him as a lamb! (John 1:29, 35). Before the baptism he referred to him as the chief priest, whose sandals he was not worthy to tie as he entered the sanctuary (Matt 3:11); but now he speaks of him as a sacrificial lamb, offered for sins. No more axe, no more fire, no more anger, simply a lamb: "Behold the lamb of God" (John 1:36).

"You don't know him," he had said previously (John 1:26), but letting it be known that he knew him, which was true since they were cousins (see Luke 1:36); and the brief dialogue introducing the baptism shows that the cousins knew each other (Matt 3:14). After the baptism, however, John says and even repeats: "I didn't know him" (John 1:31, 33). The fact is that John did not know truly, deeply, in the reality of God, the one he had baptized. What was it he discovered at the baptism to so change his way of speaking?[2]

John the Baptist was ready to meet God's messenger, the Christ, which is to say the Messiah, the king in David's line, but the one who comes up out of the waters when heaven opened was stated by God himself to be his "well-beloved Son" (Matt 3:17), and then the Holy Spirit descended upon him. At the time of the baptism, John made the discovery of the Father, the Son, and the Holy Spirit in their mysterious unity of love. God became apparent to him as all at once Father, Son, and Holy Spirit. The Baptist had never guessed at such a mystery. Nothing had prepared him for it. When he now looked at Jesus he considered him as one would consider God, and then speaks of him as he had not done previously: "I saw and bear witness that this is the Son of God" (John 1:34). Before the baptism John had never used the word "Son" to designate Jesus, far less "the Son of God"!

2. Everything developed here on the basis of events before and after Jesus' baptism requires a brief explanation of John's Gospel. In this Gospel, unlike the other three, the actual baptism of Jesus is not described; however, this does not prevent the Gospel from signaling a very clean break in the Baptist's preaching. Up to the point of John 1:28, the Baptist's words are those that precede the baptism; this is why he can say "he comes after me" (1:27), using the same terms as the other Gospels prior to the baptism (John 1:27 reiterates Mark 1:7, Matt 3:11, Luke 3:16). But from 1:29, John the Baptist says what he could not have said in truth before the baptism: "I saw the Spirit, like a dove, descend from heaven and rest upon him" (1:32). The caesura at 1:29 is marked off by the words "the next day," which, to my mind, must mean "the following day, the day after Jesus' baptism." Wonderful Gospel of John! He limits himself to speaking of "the next day", without recounting Jesus' baptism, a baptism beyond telling, it so immerses us in mystery!

Now the Baptist also speaks of Jesus by presenting him as a lamb (*amnos*), but in a way that is new when compared to the Old Testament; not as a sacrificial lamb offered by men to God, but as "*the lamb of God.*" He says this with the definite article as if speaking of a unique lamb; and "the lamb *of God*" as if the sacrifice was offered by God for humanity. The Old Testament never speaks in this way of a sacrificial victim!

Finally, the sacrifice to which John seems to be referring is indeed for sin, but this sin is surprising because it is "the sin of the world"! The Baptist could never have envisaged such a thing; he was not prepared for it. The Old Testament, as we have said, had never let it be understood that there could be a sacrifice for such a sin. Furthermore, for a sin sacrifice, the victim was never a lamb (*amnos*) but a male goat (Lev 4:23, 16:15 . . .) or a bullock (Lev 4:3, 14 . . .). Male goats were needed each year at Yom Kippur for the confession of Israel's sins; but here and now, before his very eyes, the Baptist sees a simple lamb, and on this fragile being rests the sin of the world: "behold the lamb of God who takes away the sin of the world!" (John 1:29).

How did John the Baptist come to speak like this of "the sin of the world" when there is nothing in the Scriptures that could prepare him for such an idea?

Quite simply, because Jesus himself had confessed just this sin before him. I can see no other explanation. All those John baptized had confessed their personal sins, and, perhaps, some collective sins. That is why they had all come, and this was why John was inviting baptism. When Jesus presented himself and insisted on being baptized, what was he to confess? Not his own sin, because he had none, as the New Testament tells us (1 John 3:5, Heb 4:15 . . .). He confessed the sin that nobody before had ever confessed because no one was capable of doing so since no one else had ever discerned it. Jesus confessed what he alone is able to confess, through his solidarity with the whole of mankind assumed in his incarnation. For this very sin, confessed before the Baptist, Jesus offers himself so as to take it on himself, becoming the expiatory victim, as a lamb that God alone could offer for the forgiveness of this sin. With Christ, repentance took on a depth unsuspected by the Baptist and thitherto unknown because it concerned "the sin of the whole world."

Here we have, it seems to me, the full import of what John understood on hearing the confession of Christ at his baptism; it explains the profound change in the Baptist's preaching after this baptism, which seems to have provoked such a revolution in him that I allow myself to speak of it as his "conversion."

Blessed John, to have heard what no other person heard, the confession of Christ! Blessed John, to have pondered what no one else had pondered, Christ clear-sighted enough to discern, name, and confess the sin of the world, Christ suffering compunction for this sin, Christ charging himself with this sin to free us from it through forgiveness. Gazing at the lamb, John contemplates from afar the cross, the furthest horizon of the world, the beginning of heaven.

On that day, the Baptist said nothing more. After this silence, "the next day," there are only a few words as he sees Christ come towards him: "Behold the lamb of God who takes away the sin of the world . . . ! I didn't know him . . . ! He is the Son of God . . . !" The fathomless mystery of the lamb! The mystery of the one who confessed, bore, carried away, pardoned the sin of the world! Not a goat, but a simple lamb! A mysterious weakness, strong enough nevertheless to bear the entire world with its weight of sin! Indeed, the weakness of God is stronger than humanity! (1 Cor 1:25).

## The sin of the world

What is the sin of the world? This is not "the sins" but "the sin" of the world; not the sum of all the sins perpetrated in the world; not the sum of the sins committed collectively by this or that nation, as we see in Amos, who enumerates the sins of Damascus, of Gaza, Tyre, Edom,

Ammon, and Moab, as well as those of Israel and Judah (see Amos 1 and 2); it concerns a sin that is much more profound, the sin of the world! How are we to speak of this sin, when Christ alone was able to confess it?

Perhaps we are dealing with the original and unceasingly renewed rupture inflicted on God by the whole of humanity in Adam. In Adam, effectively, "all have sinned," as Paul tells us, adding that, "by the disobedience of one man the multitude became sinful" (5:19).

Even if we manage to put words to the sin of the world, we can nonetheless never say what wounding it has inflicted on the heart of God, the immeasurable wounding to his love! The sin of the world is not a moral fault but a spiritual one which it is impossible to confess; it has too deeply bruised the heart of God. God never asked anyone to confess such a sin since no one can know his pain, even though he cries it out again and again as he seeks for humanity: "Where are you?" (Gen 3:9). There is inexpressible suffering in God, wounded and abandoned by man . . . There is no ritual foreseen in the Law of the Old Testament for the expiation of the sin of the world because no ritual could heal God's wound!

Only the Son made man could ask forgiveness of the Father since he alone is in the bosom of the Father (John 1:18) and so alone knows his pain. He alone can ask pardon, with tears of compassion and compunction. This is the prayer the Son addresses to the Father, in the silence of the Spirit of comfort.

In his humanity, Christ experienced the sin of the world, not as being culpable himself, but as its victim. He took this sin upon himself and carried it as surely as he carried the cross, being handed over, denied, and crucified by mankind as a whole. The sin of the world crucifies the lamb who then carries the world in his prayer: "Father, forgive them, for they know not what they do" (Luke 23:34).

The sin of the world is both "borne" by the lamb who was its victim, and "removed" by the lamb who thereby liberates the world; these are the two meanings of the Greek verb (*airéo*) used by John: "Behold the lamb of God who carries, who takes away the sin of the world."

The sin of the world is the most profound of collective sins. It is a sin for which we are all responsible and whose marks we all carry; but also a sin from which we are all pardoned in Christ, as attested by our baptism. It is a sin that leaves the world with a diffuse, background culpability, from which some people specifically suffer at times if I am to believe what I see in certain ones who come to visit me.

There are in fact those who are more sensitive than others to collective guilt. A sense of family guilt often presses heavily on some who have real difficulty putting into words what they are bearing. Modern psychology has made considerable and unquestionable progress on this point. But what are we to say to a culpability that runs much deeper, at the level of the sin of the world? It would be beautiful to try to put into words this diffuse guilt that weighs on some, but it would be a wasted effort. It would be lovely to seek out, investigate our past, in the collective unconscious, but we would not uncover what is deeper still, deeper than the origins of the history of humanity, since what we are looking for lies in the spiritual origin of humanity's history, with God. The world will not be able to express its sin, even while it confusedly suffers from it. It is not given to humanity to delve so profoundly into the abyss of darkness in the human heart.

All the same, to those who suffer from this sense of guilt, I believe that it helps to say that the guilt they carry is that of the whole of humanity, that it pertains to all of us and that we are all to a greater or less degree inhabited by it, incorporate as we are with the sin of the world.

I believe that it is also good to tell such people this extraordinary good news: Jesus was able to put words to the world's guilt; he was able to say what we can't; he was able to confess before God the sin of the world and take the sin away in order to free the entirety of mankind. It is extraordinary good news that forgives and heals whoever receives it in full trust and receives the confirmation of it in baptism. Indeed, Christ was able to live out the world's repentance as no one before him had done and no one after him has needed. From this repentance of Christ springs forgiveness for the entire race. Such is the formidable good news that irradiates every obscure corner of the human heart, a light which is risen for the whole of humanity, languishing though it may be in the darkness of the shadow of death.

## "Father, forgive them . . ."

What could Christ have said in the presence of John the Baptist, before going down for us into the waters of baptism? He prayed, Luke tells us (3:21), and this prayer is a blessing for us. It is only in prayer that repentance is seen; to repent is to lift up one's sin in prayer. In a prayer of repentance, a person bears his or her sin before God and places it there in his sight, waiting for his healing forgiveness. In his prayer, Christ lifted to the Father the sin of the world: "Father, forgive them, the world knows not what it does."

What Christ said on the day of his suffering (Luke 23:3), and what he continues to say today in his intercession for us (Rom 8:34), is what he had already said before John the Baptist as he confessed the sin of the world: "Father, forgive them, the world knows not what it does. I am a man with them, here to say to you what no one else ever will say because no one else knows the ill they have done you in turning away from you; no one knows the degree to which your love is wounded, or what pain there is in your heart; no one has seen the tears you have shed since the world turned away from you in its sin. The world does not know that it wounds you and crucifies me! Father, forgive them . . . ."

The prayer of the Son; a prayer of infinite tenderness which picks up and carries the world and its sin; a prayer of infinite tenderness for the wounded Father, to console his bitter tears; a prayer of infinite tenderness for us, to bring down to us the pardon that makes us alive.

How much time do we need to stay at the foot of the cross to listen to Christ pray for the forgiveness of the world? How much time is needed for us to discover the depth of his love for us? How much time to allow in the floods of this love, which leave behind the peace that he alone can give?

How much time is needed for us to stay in contemplation of Christ to understand that the Father listens silently to his prayer, this prayer he had awaited since the day he first went in search of humanity, and which now salves his wound with love? Whoever's love has been hurt, whoever has shed bitter tears, knows the consolation a plea for forgiveness brings, a consolation, indeed, that reduces us to silence. In this silence, the request for forgiveness transforms the bitter tears into tears full of sweetness, tears of joy, a joy so great that it is not possible to grant the pardon other than in silence. One who has suffered too much forgives in silence, and the forgiveness is spoken by the luminous sweetness of tears. The joy of the forgiving Father is a silent joy. How much time do we need to rest in the silence and allow the joy of the Father to flood us, the joy he has in forgiving and in cherishing this prodigal world the Son leads back to him?

When the Son came up out of the waters of baptism, the heavens were open, just as the heart of the Father is open; and out of his silence burst the word the Spirit will cause each one of us to hear: "You are my beloved child; in you I have placed all my affection" (Luke 3:22). From heaven, and for the entirety of mankind, the Father's forgiveness is now given to us, received by[3] the Son and in the Holy Spirit.

Our place is to rest in silence, in the silence of adoration in which the tears are full of the sweetness of God.

---

3. The French preposition here is *par*, which can mean "by," "with," "through"; perhaps the range of meanings is appropriate. (Trans.)

## Repentance from a medical angle _____

When we look more closely at our faults, in God's light, we realize that they are a reality in us for which our responsibility varies. Sometimes we are fully responsible, sometimes only in part, and sometimes very little; our responsibility can be so dilute as to make it seem abusive to say we are responsible at all. Though the evil is there, in us, with the pain of compunction linked to our sin, we suffer more to have been victims than as being responsible for our sin. Can we still speak of repentance? Or rather, in what terms should we confess a fault for which we feel so little responsibility?

The more collective the nature of a sin, the more our part in the responsibility is diminished and diluted. But our membership of the community certainly involves us, the joint responsibility is a burden to us and the weight of it may grind us down, in spite of ourselves; we feel trapped. When it comes to the death of Christ, for example, we could say from one point of view that we are not guilty. It all took place in our absence, nearly two thousand years ago; to accuse us of murder would be unjust. Nevertheless! From another point of view it is true that we are all responsible.

Some young Germans feel great pain because of the last world war, though they were not even born when it took place. They suffer from it as a collective sin, as a burden from which they have not managed to free themselves. It would be most unjust to accuse them of having anything to do with it! How then are we to understand the reality of the suffering linked to the sin? Are there terms in which to speak of this which are not to do with judgment?

"I will heal you of your infidelities," God said to his people (Jer 3:22). In speaking like this, God lights up and opens the way for us. The infidelities of which Jeremiah speaks are beyond doubt sins, but God nevertheless speaks of them not as acts for which to be chastised or forgiven, but as sicknesses or wounds that he proposes to heal. God moves from a juridical to a medical vocabulary, and in this way enables us to see reality in greater depth.

This change in vocabulary does not mean we have left the field of God's competence! According to the Old Testament, we have said, God is the only one truly able to forgive, and this he does in his capacity as judge. But according to the Old Testament, God is quite equally the only one able to heal (Deut 32:39). The Old Testament even denounces all physicians as charlatans, emphasizing as fact that God is the only true physician (Hos 5:13; Job 13:4). If he therefore now proposes to heal, he knows what he is talking about.

It is well known today that the majority of pedophiles suffered themselves, as children, the aggressions of a pedophile. To judge such a person for these acts is one aspect of reality, but one aspect only, that which relates to justice, but this is not the end of the matter. Beyond judgment, it must also be taken into account that their pedophilia is itself a profound suffering of which they know themselves to be victims. They know themselves to be both culpable and victims. The aspect that does not relate to justice truly requires a therapeutic approach. They also need to be treated and healed of this evil.

"I will heal your infidelities," God proclaims to his people. This word from God throws a light on our sin which allows us to understand repentance in a different way. While it reveals the reality of what lies within us, it also reveals an aspect of God that is still perhaps unknown to us. The process of repentance then takes on a new allure. It turns us toward God both as towards a judge and as towards a physician, in a subtle mix of the two that differs according to the circumstances, according to the degree of responsibility we have in the exposed wrong. The opening of our heart is at once to a judge, with a view to pardon, and to a therapist, with a view to healing.

Everything that has been said in the preceding pages concerns repentance from a juridical angle. What we now need to examine is the therapeutic factor in repentance; this concerns our sin in so far as it is an evil for which we are not culpable and that requires God's medicine. I am separating the two things for reasons of clarity, well aware that there is a mixture within us and that God's attitude towards us is both that of a judge ready to pardon and that of a physician ready to treat. Where we ourselves have trouble making the distinctions in this twofold approach, God, with his acute insight, knows perfectly well how to discern the truth. He is both a wonderful judge, able to forgive in his infinite grace, and a wonderful physician, able to heal with his incomparable knowledge.

"I will heal your infidelities," we now hear the physician saying to us.[4] We will here make no more than a few remarks on this new approach to sin.

"I will heal your infidelities"; in speaking like this, God invites us to come to him for his intervention. He invites us to open our heart and expose it to his scrutiny. The uncovering of what is wrong, the confession of our sin, the opening of our heart; these are all essential to repentance, which means that speaking of repentance remains a thoroughly just way to speak of the reality of our turning to God, but the way of experiencing this reality can be profoundly modified.

Opening one's heart before a judge always involves great trepidation, the fear of being condemned. It follows that this opening of the heart takes place without enthusiasm, with evident restraint, seeking to leave in the shadows whatever we can hide from the judge. In contrast, we open our heart to a physician most willingly, with great confidence and with the strong hope of being healed, not wishing to hide anything, so that healing be total.

The tears of a guilty person before a judge are not the tears of a sick person speaking to a physician. It is the same with compunction: the tears we shed before God are not the same, according to whether we think of him as our physician or judge.

A thief will say to the judge, "Forgive my thefts"; to the therapist he says, "Heal me of my thieving." The way we address God will also

---

4. I will not here repeat everything that was covered in *Spiritual Maladies* (*Les Maladies de la Vie Spirituelle*).

change, according to whether we address him in prayer as judge or physician.

The two ways of praying also show how the reality of our sin can be understood at different levels. To speak of thefts is to speak of acts; to speak of a compulsion to steal is to speak of one's being and so looks at a much deeper level. Acts of theft stem from the inward propensity. The healing approach to sin is therefore more profound and requires a greater light. This is another difference we can uncover between John the Baptist's and Jesus' invitation to repentance.

In his preaching, John the Baptist confines himself strictly to the juridical aspect of sin. The goal of the repentance and baptism is "the forgiveness of sins" (Mark 1:4); forgiveness relates to the mercy of the judge. The task of the physician is not forgiveness.

Further, "John did no miracle," as is confirmed by the crowds that followed him (John 10:41). This is to say that John didn't heal any sickness; he gave no sign which would suggest another aspect to God than that of judge.

"Repent, because the kingdom of heaven is at hand." When we hear the preaching of John the Baptist, the threat of judgment is real. The only recourse resides in the grace and good will of the king who will judge!

With Jesus things are different; he underlines very clearly the connection between the juridical and healing, setting to the fore the healing approach: "Which is easier to say to the paralyzed man, 'your sins are forgiven,' or to say to him, 'take up your bed and walk?' Well, so that you may know that the Son of Man has authority to forgive sins on the earth," [he said to the paralytic,] "Take up your bed and go to your home" (Mark 2:9–11). Jesus forgave and healed at the same time. He reveals God in his twin aspects of judge and physician.

The place where Jesus clearly sets forth the healing aspect is when he says to those who wish to understand, "I am not come to judge" (John 12:47). Moreover, when he speaks of his mission to sinners, he is at pains to present himself as a healer. "I am come not to call the righteous, but the sinners to repentance," he says, after having stated very clearly, "It is not the healthy who need a physician but the sick" (Luke 5:31–32). It is indeed as a healer that Jesus calls sinners to repentance. "Repent" . . . this is how he inaugurates his ministry, after which he begins to heal all those who come to him.

When the disciples of John the Baptist came to question Jesus as to his identity, he replied by advancing his healing activities, not his role as judge. "Go back and report to John all you have seen and heard: the blind recover their sight and the lame walk; the lepers are cleansed and the deaf hear; the dead are raised and the good news is announced to the poor" (Matt 11:4–5). The good news of the kingdom is so bound to the healing activity of Jesus that the one seems to be a very part of the other.

When Jesus sends out his own disciples, charging them to announce the good news of the kingdom, he states their task to be healing, not judgment: "Proclaim that the kingdom of heaven is at hand; heal the sick, raise the dead, cleanse the lepers, cast out demons"; he concludes with words that make of the disciples truly extraordinary therapists: "Freely you have received, freely give"! (Matt 10:8).

"Repent," says Jesus. Then he forgives all and heals all who come to him. Repentance takes on with him a depth and savor that there was none of with the Baptist, the savor of extraordinary good news. Yes, good news! Repentance is a healing way! "Repent," says Jesus, in the way a therapist prescribes medication. This is just what it is; to open one's heart to God and confess one's sin is to lance the wound and let the pus escape; it is to expose the wound to the cleansing action of God's forgiveness. The process might be painful and provoke tears, but this doesn't stop it from being salutary, or God's forgiveness from being a true healing balm that soothes and reestablishes good health.

The good news we hear from Jesus' mouth has the power to relieve all disquietude. Where we don't always know ourselves to distinguish, in the complexity of our hearts, which things pertain to the judge and which to the physician, God makes no mistakes. For us everything is linked, but he knows perfectly what in our sin relates to justice and pardon, and what to therapy and healing. We can truly open our hearts to him in full confidence.

What, then, is the goal of repentance—the pardon of the judge or the healing of the physician? Both at once, in an inseparable way; God is at once both judge and healer. The more we conceive of God as the healer of our souls the more confident and open will be our repentance, knowing that the healing we receive from him will be achieved through his forgiveness. Furthermore, we will have no fear to find ourselves in the presence of our judge since we are persuaded that he is forgiving and he brings us healing.

The healing and pardon of God result in the subtle and wonderful blend of feeling we call peace.

## Repentance in the hands of the creator

The closer a person approaches to God, the more profoundly he or she sees the darkness of his or her own heart. We will now look a little more closely at this spiritual truth.

As we move towards encounter with God along the road of repentance, our prayer deepens to the point where, one day, in this growing closeness to God, we no longer address him as judge, saying "I have committed this or that sin," but as healer, saying to him, "I am a sinner." In our prayer we seek less to name our faults than to expose to God our sinful condition. What Judas said to the chief priests was limited to the act of which he knew himself to be guilty: "I have sinned," he confessed. In contrast the tax collector of the parable looked more deeply into his life and addressed God saying, "I am a sinner" (Luke 18:13). The tax collector's gaze goes much further than that of Judas. It is Jesus who gives this example of the tax collector; he doesn't enumerate his sins before God but rather commits his sinful being to him. This is something we also understand in the mouth of Abba Matoes, who formulates in the same terms the axiom we mentioned previously: "The closer a man draws to God, the more he sees himself as a sinner" (Sentence 514). Abba Matoes was right; it's not "the more he sees his sins," but, "the more he sees himself as a sinner." These are the terms in which Peter expressed himself to Jesus at their first meeting: "Lord, depart from me, for I am a sinner" (Luke 5:8).

If humanity refers to itself as a sinner, this is not to be understood as an ontological[5] statement. Man and woman did not indeed emerge as a sinner from the hands of their creator. On the contrary, we say "he is a sinner" as we would say of someone, "he is sick." It does not constitute part of his being but is accidental and passing. Humanity has become a sinner as one "becomes sick." Humanity came from God's hands good, "very good" even, according to what God affirms after creating man and woman (Gen 1:31). In what followed, however, humanity became a sinner, and that is what it is in relation to God today, and it is thus that healing from God becomes necessary.

"I am a sinner," Peter said, like the tax collector. The depth of this avowal varies according to the increasing light received through God's approach. The sharpness of our insight increases with the light to the point where, one day, humanity says, with the psalmist: "I am sinful from my birth, and in sin did my mother conceive me" (51:7).[6]

For sure, insight beyond the ordinary is needed if we are to see our own life back to the moment of conception; or rather, a very particular light is needed, that of God, to be so illuminated. When he attains such lucidity about himself in prayer, the psalmist does not turn towards God as to a judge to seek pardon, but more towards a physician to seek healing. The verbs "pardon" and "heal" are notably absent from this great psalm of repentance; instead, the psalmist has another request to make of God, for an intervention so deep that he addresses God as creator: "*Create* in me a clean heart" (51:12).

5. *Ontology*, the study of being; thus, ontological, the root nature of a thing. (Trans.)

6. There is a very fine, detailed exposition of Psalm 51 in the author's book *Happy are the Pure in Heart*. (Trans.)

This is a wonderful prayer, agreeing with another great affirmation of the Old Testament, which is, that, as God is the only one who can really forgive and heal, so he is also the only one who can really create (the verb *bârâ'*, "to create," only has God as its subject).

More profound than occasional sin is sin that has become habitual as a result of repetition across time. The psalmist does more than discover in himself this or that long-standing habitual attitude; he goes all the way back to the very origin of his life and discovers a sort of congenital malformation. In this prayer he only speaks before God of his own case; he isn't intending to expose truth of a general nature. He does not propose to speak of what may be in others' lives! How would it be possible to see so deeply into others? He stops at saying what he has seen in his own life, what he discerns in himself with God's help.

A person whom God has enabled to see so far into his or her life and to repent to such a depth, has received from God the knowledge of him as a creator able to create a new heart, a pure heart; this is still good news for us today.

Whoever, indeed, discovers that they are a sinner from their mother's breast, might well despair and believe themselves subjected to an ineluctable fate. This psalm opens a new horizon, of faith and hope in a creative act from God; a new horizon, confirmed in this word from Jeremiah, "Before I fashioned you in your mother's womb, I knew you" (1:5). Wonderful good news: I may well have been a sinner from the start, but this is not set in stone; God still controls the situation. "Before your conception, I knew you," says God. Putting it another way, before sin even became a part of your life, I already knew you, which is to say, I loved you (in Hebrew "I know you" is a synonym for "I love you," above all when spoken by God). Before your life was marked by sin, it was marked by my love; your sin is no more than dross in the fire of my love, which cleanses your life.

God's love is deeper than our sin; where sin abounds, love superabounds. Anyone who goes right down to the deepest place of their sin will there still find themselves faced with the love of God! Anyone who goes down to the deepest place of pain, will there still meet with the loving look of God! No road of repentance is a dead end; each such road immerses us in the fathomless love of God! There is nothing so wonderful as this good news.

The author of Psalm 51 knows himself to be a sinner from his mother's womb, but this does not cause him to despair. He knows that he is incapable of remedying something that has always been so; but he also knows just as well that God can do anything, create anything. A person may despair of their own self, but not of God. In his repentance, the psalmist throws himself into the hands of the creator, who is now his whole expectation in every way since, in God's presence, he himself is nothing . . . nothing!

When God creates, he starts with nothing. The psalmist knows it; this is why when he asks God to create he recognizes himself as a zero.

It may be that one day we recognize ourselves to be nothing in the hands of God. To then open our heart before him is to recognize that our heart is nothing, that our life, our faith, our love . . . that it is all no longer anything—"without form and void," as was the earth before God created (Gen 1:2). A day may come when, in the intensity of God's light, in the intensity of his fire, there is nothing of us left. Everything is burnt up and consumed; even the tears are gone! Then repentance is summed up in these few words, no more perhaps than a thought, a look or a simple sigh: "O God, create in me a clean heart . . . starting with this nothing that I am!"

Our legal, penitential language may be worn out, and our medical, healing vocabulary too, but though we have nothing left but silence, there still remains our gaping wound open to God, our emptiness thirsting for love; there remains the nothingness of our being, from which starting point the love of God can bring to birth our new being and transform our nothing into a new creature.

"I am a sinner from my mother's womb," says the psalmist. "Create in me a clean heart," he is able to ask in his prayer. His confidence in God is so great that he already sees himself as a new creature, ready to speak its first words: "Lord, open thou my lips." As God opens the lips of every newborn, so he will open those of his new creature. The psalmist knows that the moment God opens his lips, his prayer will be simply a song of love: "Lord, open thou my lips, and my mouth will show forth thy praise" (Ps 51:17).

Before he has so much as finished his prayer the psalmist is full of a certitude that enthralls him in wonderment: "the heart that is broken in repentance you have not despised" (51:19).

The measureless love of God . . .

# CHAPTER 5

# The Repentance Preached
# by the Disciples

A FTER LOOKING AT THE preaching of John the Baptist and Jesus, it now remains for us to examine that of the disciples. They too were instructed to preach repentance, and the Gospels show us that this is just what they did, as attested by the simple statement in Mark, "They went out and preached that everyone should repent" (6:12).

What we learn from this verse concerns the very first mission of the disciples. Jesus told them precisely what they were to proclaim, but we know nothing about the manner they adopted in accomplishing their mission. The Gospels leave us no other detail than that "they went out and preached that people should repent"! How are we to preach repentance today? What can the New Testament tell us to help us fulfill our mission? This is the question I would now like to investigate.

Since the Gospels say nothing about the way in which the disciples set about their preaching of repentance, we need to turn to the book of Acts to learn a little more in this area; and, indeed, this book proves to be very precious.

"Repent," Peter proclaims to the crowd on the day of Pentecost (2:38). "Repent," he says again a few days later (3:19). "Repent" is said a final time by the same apostle to Simon the magician some time later (8:22). These are the three calls to repentance reported in Acts. The preaching of repentance is well and truly present at the dawn of church history, so there is plenty here from which to draw teaching for ourselves today; these three occasions are sufficient encouragement for us to follow the steps of the apostles and take up the preaching baton.

Did all the apostles preach repentance? Certainly! This is what they had all preached in the course of their first mission, before Christ's death, and they had all similarly been sent by him following his resurrection. It is curious to note that in this new mission, in the church's first days, the invitations to repentance are found only in Peter's mouth. The apostles had all been commissioned by Jesus to the same mission, but only Peter is described as putting it into practice. It's not that the author of Acts seems to want to discredit the others, but rather he gives a clear impression of wishing to present Peter as the preacher of repentance *par excellence*. The focus on this apostle has a great teaching in it for us.

Peter is precisely the one disciple who received the most beautiful invitation from Christ to repentance. This took place, as you remember, on the night of Peter's denial. The method Jesus adopted to thrust his disciple onto the road of repentance is altogether extraordinary. It was accomplished in silence, with just one steadfast look after the cock had crowed. Jesus said nothing, but Peter understood completely. The silence of Christ! A silent sermon! To be exact it was Christ's look that spoke, more than his silence! Putting things together—it was his silent look!

This sermon in a gaze made of Peter the perfect penitent; it remained for him a point of reference, as it is for us too, even if it is impossible for us to reproduce; impossible since Christ has not looked into our eyes in quite this way!

One silent look and that was enough. This silent preaching, to me, is exemplary in the way it conveys its contents—it is full of the humble and modest love of Christ. There is no need for long discourses to invite repentance; the sin to be confessed is revealed by the delicate love that Jesus evinces.

An exemplary sermon and an action that is no doubt beyond our scope! Also, however, an outlook we should constantly bear in mind.

What the repentant Peter had drawn from his source in Christ, he is now able to pass on, preaching repentance in his turn. It is not for nothing that the author of Acts chose Peter as his model preacher of repentance. He teaches us that the person best able to preach repentance to others is the one who has first experienced it himself in depth, in a look from Christ.

Peter, then, begins to preach, but not in silence this time! Silence would not be enough; his words will make explicit what he received in the look of his Lord. We will pause a little over these words because they are particularly illuminating.

The denial which was Peter's guilty fault so marked him that his preaching is marked by it too. "You *denied* the Christ," he says to the crowd (Acts 3:13–14). The word chosen by Peter clearly shows how deeply impacted he was by his own story. Nevertheless he doesn't focus on himself. There is no account of his own sin or his own repentance; not even the forgiveness he received. Peter says nothing of his own experience; the crowd knows nothing of the denial of which he was guilty. This doesn't prevent Peter from drawing on his own experience to find words that will touch the crowd to the point it sees itself in them. It was indeed the reality; it is correct to say that the crowd had denied the very one they had acclaimed as king on "Palm Sunday." Peter was right to speak of the crowd's "denial." With this word the people become conscious of their own sin; they had acclaimed Christ, recognizing him as their king, but in Pilate's presence they had denied him: "We have no king other than Caesar!" (John 19:15).

Preaching repentance means connecting the other person with his sin without stating it, in words that are his own, and with the humility of one who knows his own sinfulness.

Having engaged in denial himself and thoroughly aware of his own sin, Peter does not judge the sinners he is now addressing; there is no condescension in what the apostle says. One who has sinned himself can only continue to be humble in his preaching of repentance. Of what could he be proud when he had denied the very one to whom he had said, "You are the Christ, the Son of the living God"? (Matt 16:16). Humility—this is the impression we take away from Peter's discourse. Without humility, the preaching of repentance crushes the other and risks plunging him into despair. Peter's crushes nobody and pushes no one to despair; the preaching turns people back to God, opening the way to forgiveness.

"You denied the Holy One, the Just . . . the Prince of life . . ." (Acts 3:14). Peter multiplies the terms used to designate Christ in order to focus the crowd's attention on him. What Peter sets out before the crowd as their sin is not a moral failing or a scorned law, but a victim, a person: Christ. The sin is less a twisting of a rule, even if the rule is the Law of God, but rather a wound inflicted on Christ, an offense to God's love, a rupture in relationship with the Lord.

"Repent, you who denied Christ," Peter says to the crowd. He might well have said, "Let us repent, we who have denied him"! A few days earlier this is what he would have said; if he doesn't do so now it is because he knows his sin is forgiven. He knows he is always loved by the one he denied, and in turn loves the one who forgave him. Peter doesn't instance this in his preaching of repentance, but the love is alive in him, and it is the strength behind his words. The power of preaching is not only in the words used, but also in the force of love with which the words are spoken. "Repent," says Peter with this love inside him. As he thus shows the way to God's heart, Peter is showing the people the way of forgiveness that God alone provides through the one who is now alive and risen.

The core of Peter's preaching is the good news of the resurrection of Christ. It is this good news that lights up the call to repentance. In Peter's mouth, the invitation to repent is inseparable from the proclamation of this good news. "Repent," he says, "because the one who was dead is now alive. The way of repentance is radiant with the light of the resurrected Christ."

# CHAPTER 6

# God's Repentance

"Repent," was John the Baptist's message to the people. "Repent," said Jesus in turn. "Repent," the Apostle Peter takes up the refrain once again. This appeal is made in different accents, but the goal is always the same, to reestablish relations of love between man and God. On the road to God's heart, repentance is so important that it is prioritized by these three preachers; we are given the opportunity to grab hold of it, to put it into practice and thus draw near to God.

"Repent." Very strangely, if we look for this plural imperative in the Old Testament, it is not to be found! Neither is it there in the singular. No one in the Old Testament uses the phrase, even though so many of the prophets called out to the people to invite them in one form or another to return to God. Where we don't hear in the Old Testament the call to repentance, we often hear a call to conversion: "be converted" (Isa 31:6, Jer 3:14, Ezek 14:6, Joel 2:2, Zech 1:3 . . .), which is to say, "retrace your steps," "turn back to God," "change your behavior." The call to conversion is elaborated at every period and in every way by the prophets to make the people understand God's thirst for true relationship, for love relationship with his people.

By preaching conversion rather than repentance the prophets were inviting a change in behavior, not the deeper change repentance represents, that is, a change of thinking, of feeling, a change at heart level, grounded in love.

This first fact about repentance in the Old Testament is accompanied by a second that is still more astonishing, but which helps explain the first.

This second fact is that the repentance most at issue is not humanity's but God's! The Old Testament indeed speaks of God's repentance. When it speaks like this it is not fleetingly, not just in some one verse; nor is it found only in archaic verses which could be considered naïve anthropomorphisms; nor from a somewhat avant-garde pen that would make the theme a little eccentric! No, God's repenting appears in the Psalms, in the Pentateuch, and the prophets. The theme is there, substantially present, and we need now, reader friend, to take some time to consider this closely.

You will note that I have waited until the end of the book to go into this, despite it being a bigger issue in the Old Testament than the repentance of humanity. It's even apparent in the Old Testament that God's repentance is of primary concern as it relates to humanity, in the sense that humanity's repentance relies on God's. As you see, I have left until last that which comes first. This is not because I have wished to keep the best for the conclusion, but simply because this subject, I would have to confess, plunges me into a deep silence! It is only in silence, indeed, that I am able to consider the idea of God repenting . . .

Anyone who is repenting opens their heart! How are we to think about this, of God opening his heart in the pain of repentance? To face up to this requires infinite love on our part, a love that is beyond me, to which I aspire, but of which I fall so far short that there is nothing for me in my poverty but silence.

It is not possible to speak of God repenting without weighing each word with great care, without having prayed over each word. I can do little more than stammer, asking God to forgive me for venturing beyond silence . . .

Another reason for leaving the discussion of God's repentance till last is to allow an ensuing time of silence, the time needed to ponder the infinite love God demonstrates in his repentance.

In order to sully this important topic as little as possible I will no more than touch on it before leaving you to your thoughts and prayer, or indeed, very simply, leaving you with God . . .

## God does not repent . . .

Two passages in the Old Testament (Num 23:19 and 1 Sam 15:29) clearly affirm that God does not repent, for the very simple reason that he is not a human who would need to repent. This leaves one to think that repentance could not be incident to God, and even that it would be close to blasphemous to think that God could repent! These two verses certainly need to be examined very closely, since the rest of the Old Testament seems to contradict them. Both the verses need to be seen in their context to be properly understood.

"God is not a man that he should repent" (Num 23:19): this is the phrase addressed by the seer Balaam to Balak, the king of Moab, who had commanded him to curse his neighbor, the people of Israel. Balaam was ready to do what was asked of him; nonetheless, God had decided differently and commanded Balaam to pronounce words of blessing, and it is one of these blessings that contains the affirmation that "God is not a human that he should repent," and so the meaning, in the present case, is that he does not repent of his blessing.

These words are fundamental to understanding the rest of the Old Testament: God does not repent of his blessing, which is to say that he does not renounce his love and that he will not renounce it, whatever happens. It was good that someone would affirm this at the outset of Israel's history. It was even a good thing that it be said by a stranger, stood on a mountain on the frontier of Israel, his gaze fixed on this little people: "God blesses his people and does not repent of his blessing." The non-repentance of God is a sign here of the faithfulness of his love.

The second text (1 Sam 15) places us a little later in the history of Israel, at the beginning of the kingdom. It fell to the prophet to say again, "God is not a human that he should repent." The context is entirely different. Samuel says it to King Saul, who has just been rejected by God because Saul had been unfaithful to him. Samuel expresses himself very solemnly, as if to affirm a truth from all eternity about God: "God is not a human that he should repent!" The tone is solemn, certainly, but Samuel knew something else about God, and what he knew was just the opposite! In fact the very night before his encounter with Saul, Samuel had heard God say to him, "I repent of having made Saul king, because he has turned away from me and failed to observe my word" (15:11). This confession of God to his prophet moved Samuel profoundly, as the remainder of this verse tells us: "Samuel was angry and spent the night crying out to the Lord." This night of anger speaks of the prophet's deep confusion. Samuel does not understand God's repentance or why he had rejected Saul, not knowing what had passed between God and the king. Then, during this night of anger, God unveils to Samuel Saul's wrongs. The next day, when the prophet and king meet, Saul again begins to lie to Samuel and persist in his wrongdoing. It is then that Samuel tells Saul of his rejection by God, telling him at the same time that God would not go back on this rejection, given that "God is not a man that he should repent"!

God loves his people and in his love gave them a king. Notwithstanding, still out of love for his people, God had now to reject the unfaithful king and give the people another king, one after God's heart. God would not rescind this rejection, and we see clearly that the non-repentance of God is again the sign of his faithfulness in his love for Israel.

Saul is unaware that he will not see Samuel again, and that Samuel will have no desire that he should. Saul doesn't know the extent of Samuel's attachment to him, how wounded he is, his pain at Saul's rejection, and also his pain to see the king have so little regard for the love of God. How was he to act towards this king who had no wish to understand God's love? Not knowing what to do, and to hide his tears of pain, Samuel departs and never sees Saul again. Samuel concludes the account with a last word on God's repentance: "Samuel never saw Saul again as long as he lived; and Samuel mourned over Saul because the Lord repented to have established him king over Israel" (15:35).

"Samuel mourned over Saul . . . !" What Samuel in his tears was perhaps unaware of is that God himself may also have mourned, wounded much more than Samuel in his love for Saul . . . When a prophet mourns, God is mourning!

God's repentance is therefore a reality, the reality of a God of love who is faced with the inconsistency of men, the inconsistency of those who have so little regard for his love. It was in love that God had made Saul a king for his people. It was in love that he rejected this lying king in order to give the people a king worthy of the name. As for this liar, he was a man and as a man he could repent and seek God and his love. Saul made a pretense of repenting that day before Samuel, but he did it to save face and Samuel was not fooled. The prophet withdrew to grieve in secret over the king, leaving him to God. Saul did not repent; had he done so he would perhaps have found that God too was weeping over his lying king . . . The end of Saul is altogether as tragic as that of Judas; he too sank into suicide, but without having sought the way of repentance.

The remainder of the Old Testament shows God traversing the road of repentance from one end to the other in search of man. What infinite love, the humble love of God! It was not until after he had thoroughly trodden this route that God decided to send a prophet, John the Baptist, and then his Son, to proclaim to all, "Repent."

"God is not a human that he should repent": this statement is not repeated in the Old Testament or in the New because, since the time of Samuel in particular, God had clearly let the reverse be known. So, to say that God does not repent would be the affirmation of a principle, a dogma, good only for enclosing God within a particular image, a sort of brand name. God, however, has no brand name to defend; he loves and that is an end to it! In his love and because of his love, he is led to repent.

## . . . and God repents

You remember that at the outset of the process of repentance there is some word or event that brings a consciousness of a wrong that has been done. Well, the same thing takes place with God; thus, for example, the psalmist recounts how one day God repented after hearing the supplications of the Israelites, and it was indeed their supplications which triggered his repentance: "They were obstinate in their rebellion and sank deeper into their sin. But he regarded them in their distress, when he heard their pleas. He remembered his covenant with them, and, in his great kindness, he repented . . ." (Ps 106.43–45).

It is not that God repents of a fault he has committed! It is the people who were at fault! Nevertheless, from the people's fault a situation of oppression was born that caused them to cry out and that would have continued without God's intervention. God would have deemed himself at fault had he not intervened! He could have been accused of abandoning his people, and now, rather than seem "at fault," God repents. This repentance is a wonderful manifestation of his kindness, at which the psalmist marvels.

Repentance, we have seen, takes place in the pain of compunction. Just what is there of this in God's repentance? The Old Testament is extremely discreet about God's suffering, so there is nothing surprising in seeing that the texts that speak of God's repentance are silent as to his compunction. There is one, however, which evokes it, very soberly but just enough to shed some light on the matter.

The text is that which relates the story of the flood. People had become so evil that God repented of having created them. At this point, the text tells us, "He was afflicted in his heart." This affliction of God's that is alongside his repentance, and is finely stated to be "in his heart," this is compunction: "The Lord repented to have made man on the earth; he was afflicted in his heart" (Gen 6:6).[1]

What more can be said about this pain of God, since he spoke of it to no one? God keeps his pain to himself! His sorrow is simply in the same measure as his love for his creature, which is to say, it is beyond measure! It is a fathomless suffering which we can only approach in silence . . . Who could provide any balm for this wound?

Noah! What a wonderful text! There is a glimmer of hope . . .

"Noah found grace in the eyes of the Lord" (Gen 6:8). From this man a new humanity will be born, one which will perhaps respond to God's love.

The vital stage of repentance is the opening of the heart and the confession to the offended party. The account of the flood concludes with a decision from God that strongly resembles a confession; nevertheless, the text is very clear that God's thoughts at this point are retained "in his heart." Clearly Noah was informed of them, but we note however that there is no openly stated confession. The narrator is very fine in the way he spares God's honor by passing over the confession; instead he goes immediately to God's decision not to repeat what he had done: "The Lord said *in his heart*, 'I will not curse the earth again because of man, because the thoughts in the heart of man are wicked from his youth up. I will not again smite every living thing as I have done'" (8:21).

If the narrator dares not describe God as confessing to Noah the evil he has inflicted on mankind as culpable, it is a biblical text, nonetheless, in which God himself does say what the narrator dares not write! This is an overwhelming text of love and humility, one of the

---

1. This "affliction" of God's goes so far beyond our understanding that the first Greek translators, before our era, preferred to alter the text. The very idea of God's repentance was insupportable to them, which is why instead of saying, "The Lord repented to have made man on the earth; he was afflicted in his heart," we find in the Greek of the Septuagint: "God was concerned about having made man on the earth and considered the matter deeply."

texts where God is revealed in a love and humility to which nothing else can be likened.

The scene changes and we see the ruins of Jerusalem still smoking after the disaster inflicted on Israel by the Babylonian troops. The people remaining are reduced to a mere handful, and this small group of survivors come to ask of the prophet Jeremiah a word from the Lord (Jer 42). God has his hand in Jerusalem's disaster; it is his reaction to the multiple sins of the people, an invitation to repentance. The survivors seem to demonstrate a good disposition towards God, and say they are prepared to do whatever he tells them. Jeremiah therefore intercedes before God in favor of these few who have escaped. The Lord does not immediately respond to the prophet's prayer; he delays. He delays for a considerable time! The reply comes at the end of "ten days," the text specifies (42:7). Why such slowness in responding? Simply because God is going to say something he has never said before, and do what he has never before done. While he is entitled to await the repentance of the survivors among his rebellious people, God will himself confess what he has never before confessed! Moved by the suffering of the escaped handful, the Lord opens his heart with incomparable humility. This is what God says, the Lord of lords, to a few miserable survivors of a rebellious people: "I repent of the evil that I have inflicted upon you" (42:10).

What infinite love and measureless humility! Not one man among this people had accepted the need to repent! Not one! As God had earlier stated to his prophet: "I am attentive and listening; they don't speak as they should; no one repents of his wickedness" (8:6). Yet right here, with this very people who refuse to repent, God sets out alone along the road of repentance.

It would have been easy for God to justify himself before his people, explaining to them the meaning of the evil that the fall of Jerusalem represented. The evil they underwent is nothing but pure justice, the logical outcome of the people's rebellion, of their disobedience to God. It would also have been easy for God to demonstrate that it was in love he had punished them. Is it not the case that "he who loves well, chastises well"? Instead, after ten days of silence, he neither argues nor justifies himself; he pursues a way that reveals his extraordinary humility: "I repent of the evil which I have inflicted upon you . . . ." The humility of God is to be measured by his love; it is without limit!

How could one not be reconciled to such a God? After repentance and confession to the offended party, there ought to follow reconciliation through the granting of forgiveness. How though did the people react to the repentance of their God? They paid no attention to it! Worse still, they did the opposite of what the Lord advised them. They had promised Jeremiah they would do whatever God told them, but their good resolutions were no more than a show; they merely hid the depth of their disregard for the Lord.

God says nothing of his pain! Before such disregard, suffering has only one refuge, silence.

One person alone on that day was able to draw near to God in his solitude, Jeremiah. He too was silent; compassion at times has silence as its sole recourse.

But we will leave aside the pride that refuses to set foot on the road of repentance and scorns the one who does; we will ponder instead the humility of God.

How humble is this God who considers himself blameworthy for punishing his guilty people and confesses this to them.

It is a humility without bounds that immerses us in wonderment.

Yet the humility of God goes still further! Not only does God repent before men for what he had done to them, but even repents of what he had only thought to do. Who would be at pains to confess the ill that had passed through his mind but had not committed? Not very many for sure! But God does repent of this too; as he says again to Jeremiah: "Perhaps they will listen to me and turn each one from his own wicked way; then I would repent of the evil which I thought to inflict upon them" (26:3). Only love could lend humility such infinite depth . . .

God is so humble that he even accepts the idea of listening to someone who preaches repentance to him! In the Old Testament, God had never invited men to repent by telling them to "repent," but he in fact listens to a man telling him to do just that!

This took place on a mountain, in the one-on-one intimacy between God and Moses, his friend, when the people wounded God in his love by making a golden calf. "Moses pacified the LORD his God, saying to him, 'Why, O LORD, is your anger inflamed against your people who you brought up out of Egypt by your great power and strong hand? Why should the Egyptians say that it is for their wickedness that you brought them out to kill them here in the mountains and make them perish from off the face of the earth? Turn back from the heat of your anger, and repent of the evil which you wish to inflict upon your people . . .'" (Exod 32:11–12).

If there was anyone to whom Moses should be preaching repentance it was the people, and Moses was well placed to do this, yet this is not what he does. He knows the heart of humanity too well! Instead he prefers to turn to the heart of God and say to him what no one else would ever have dared to say: "Repent . . . !"

How long was the silence that followed this audacious speech? I don't know!

Moses was silent!

Heaven and earth were silent, awaiting the response of God . . . What a silence!

God receives his friend's proposal in silence. He doesn't reply; he doesn't justify himself. Humbly, the Lord takes the path of repentance, the text relates without adding a single word of commentary: "The Lord repented of the evil that he had purposed to inflict on his people" (32:14).

The only commentary to be made is in the silence of contemplation; a contemplation in which the bitter tears of repentance for the sin which wounds God mingle with the sweet tears of adoration.

Moses is silent and ponders the Humble One who silently treads the way of repentance . . .

"Repent, repent," cried John the Baptist in the midst of the wilderness . . .

Then John, too, was silent, as he pondered the Humble One who in silence came down into the waters of repentance . . .

God had never been so close . . .